Sook's Cookbook

UPDATED EDITION

Sook's Cookbook

Memories and Traditional Receipts from the Deep South

MARIE RUDISILL

With a Foreword by JOHN T. EDGE

Louisiana State University Press)|(Baton Rouge

Designer: Barbara Neely Bourgoyne
Typeface: Myriad Pro, display; Chapparel Pro, text
Printer and binder: Thomson-Shore, Inc.

Library of Congress Cataloging-in-Publication Data
Rudisill, Marie.
  Sook's cookbook : memories and traditional receipts from the Deep
South / Marie Rudisill, with a foreword by John T. Edge. — Updated ed.
      p. cm.
  Includes index.
  ISBN 978-0-8071-3379-8 (pbk. : alk. paper) 1. Cookery, American—
Southern style. I. Faulk, Sook, 1871–1946. II. Title.
  TX715.2.S68R83 2009
  641.5975—dc22
                                                          2008021299

The paper in this book meets the guidelines for permanence
and durability of the Committee on Production Guidelines for
Book Longevity of the Council on Library Resources. ∞

To the memory of Sook Faulk and Truman Capote

—M. R.

Contents

Foreword

A house filled with the smells of good cooking is one of the things all
of us remember from our childhoods, from the world we grew up in.
Memories of food, all our deepest memories, are like musical phrases
in an intricate symphony: they come in modestly, swell to importance,
fade into oblivion, and later return, often livelier than they were before.

MARIE RUDISILL

In December of 2000, Marie Rudisill appeared on the *Tonight Show
with Jay Leno*. As the cameras rolled, the eighty-nine-year-old taught
Leno and Mel Gibson to bake a proper fruitcake, the sort of confec-
tion that Rudisill learned to make while still a child, skittering about
the kitchen of her aunt, Sook Faulk, in Monroeville, Alabama.

Rudisill had just written a book, *Fruitcake: Memories of Truman
Capote and Sook,* and the appearance was understood to be a market-
ing stunt, an invitation to take a seat on that famous couch and sell.
Rudisill played the crowd. She chided Leno for dismissing fruitcakes
as leaden doorstops. She cajoled and caterwauled. She was sassy. She
was bawdy. And she was a hit.

Soon, she signed on as the show's advice columnist. In a recurring
segment, "Ask the Fruitcake Lady," Rudisill—dressed in a black suit,
gray hair pinned in a bun, fingernails lacquered red—addressed matters of fidelity, grooming, etiquette, and more. She was combative.
She did not suffer fools. In the process, Rudisill charmed America. Or,
at least, she charmed the goodly portion of America that watched the
Tonight Show.

Rudisill's television performances were camp. But her outré southern
pedigree came honestly. She inherited it. "It's a weird family, I kid you

not," Rudisill once said of the extended web of Faulk kin. "But it's a fabulous family."

Born Edna Marie Faulk, Marie Rudisill was the sister of writer Truman Capote's mother, née Lillie Mae Faulk. Capote called Rudisill "Aunt Tiny." Later in life, after one of their many tiffs, she took to calling him "Nephew Nasty."

After her sister died, Rudisill helped raise Capote, who was thirteen years younger than she, in the Faulk family's Monroeville household, a dominion of spinsters ruled by Jenny Faulk, Sook's strong-willed sister. In the decades to come, that household and that southern Alabama town served as the inspiration for much of what Capote and, by extension, Rudisill, wrote. (In that same town, at that same time, Nell Harper Lee, a childhood playmate of Capote, lived the storyline that would become the basis of *To Kill a Mockingbird*.)

Rudisill spent her formative years in Monroeville, but she was not a child of the provinces. During a long life that ended in 2006 at the age of ninety-five, Marie Rudisill bounded about the country. Along with her husband, James Rudisill, and their son, Jim, she lived in Branchville, South Carolina, and New York City as well as Dallas, North Carolina, and, finally, Hudson, Florida.

She worked as an antiques dealer, specializing in paperweights; a writer who penned hundreds of articles for newspapers and home and garden magazines, mostly on antiques; and as an author, who published eight books, including a children's cookbook, *Critter Cakes and Frog Tea: Tales and Treats from the Emerald River* (1994), and a tell-all memoir, *The Southern Haunting of Truman Capote* (2000).

In the decades to come, she will be remembered best for the book you hold in your hands. Originally published in 1989, *Sook's Cookbook* began as a collaboration with her famous nephew. But the final methodology—using nineteenth-century plantation daybooks for inspiration and pairing recipes with profiles of family and community cooks—was her own.

Rudisill unearthed culinary treasures that were unsuspected. But *Sook's Cookbook* is more than a roster of recipes for green olive jambalaya, watermelon rind preserves, and poinsettia cake. It's best appreciated as a portrait of place, and, more important, a portrait of people. Rudisill paid homage to the sort of cooks who had rarely been heralded. In the process, she wrote one of the most compelling regional cookbooks of the later half of the twentieth century.

Herein you will meet Sook, made famous in Capote's story, "A Christmas Memory." Rudisill describes her as "a frail little woman with skin drawn taut across her cheekbones, almost translucent, like a fragile teacup held to the light." She was, in the eyes of Rudisill, "happy and lighthearted" when "cooking on the big old black wood stove. That stove would roar, summer or winter, no matter. When questioned about the terrible heat on the hottest days, Sook's stock answer was, 'And who cares, pray tell?'"

And you will meet Victorio, the Native American who ran a fish-camp and bootlegging operation where Sook bought whiskey, a key ingredient in her fruitcakes. "The big Indian loved them," recalls Rudisill. "He would pull up a crate and a bottle of his moonshine whiskey and eat big chunks of the cake while slugging away at his bottle."

A pantheon of African American cooks get their due, too. (Rudisill was one of the early white writers to acknowledge their acumen.) Like the putative mammy of the family, Aunt Pallie (named for the goddess of wisdom, Pallas Athene.) "Aunt Pallie's babies had a taste for everything from the mother's table," writes Rudisill. "If she could get away with it, [she] tied a bag of sassafras around their necks for protection."

And Corrie Wolff, a Louisiana native whose cabin, Rudisill writes, was "the sort of place children begged to be allowed to go to eat and to sleep on the deep shuck-filled mattress and sweet down pillows, the kind of place where a child could poke a hole in the side of a cold biscuit and pour molasses in it or sit smothered in the big bed and eat a fill of collard greens with the pot liquor and corn pone. . . ."

And then there was Little Bit, the primary cook in the Faulk household. "When it came to cooking," Rudisill wrote, "Little Bit had no equal." Although Rudisill does not share Little Bit's family name, she does honor her life work by way of a description that is playful and robust. In a time when most cookbooks rendered so-called hired help as mere caricatures, Rudisill gave tentative voice and stature to the men and women who claimed the kitchens of Monroeville, Alabama, as their own. Upon reflection and in anticipation of this new edition of *Sook's Cookbook*, that may be her signal achievement.

"She was a huge woman with the agility of a Siamese cat," Rudisill writes. "She had a deep scar running across her left cheek from the tip of her ear to her chin. But it didn't detract from her oval cameo face or her long coal-black hair parted in the middle and combed over her temples. For so slender a woman, her mouth as startlingly full and red-lipped. Little Bit's love for men was no secret. She loved to talk about her love life, and at the drop of a hat, she would say, 'There's no sweeter place to lay for love than in a fresh haymow. Gawd, just smellin' that mixture of horse and hay is purely like bitin' into an unexpected pepper.'"

A bite unexpected. One might say the same of Marie Rudisill's wonderful cookbook. Of her take on her native South. Of her queer and unconventional life.

John T Edge, Oxford, Mississippi, 2007

N.b.: I admire *Sook's Cookbook*. And I'm very pleased that LSU Press has brought it back into print. I cook from it fairly often. (One of my favorites is Little Bit's recipe for bacon popovers.) But my memories of Marie Rudisill will always be more personal, more idiosyncratic, more, well, Marie. To wit:

When my son, Jess, was born, Marie was one of the first to send a gift. The house was overflowing with board books and rattles, smocks and booties. Marie had the presence of mind to think, not of our newborn, but of my wife. When the box arrived, wrapped in a gauze of chiffon paper and baby blue ribbons, Blair tore in to find a lovely—and very old-fashioned—trove of perfumes and lotions and potions from White Diamonds by Elizabeth Taylor. Blair teared up. So did I.

After I helped with a book deal negotiation, Marie phoned. She was effusive in her thanks. "I'll do anything for you," Marie said, her tone raspy, her timbre bright. I was hoping that meant one of her fruitcakes would soon arrive by parcel post. But Marie had other ideas. After a three beat pause, she added, "Except sex." A hail of cackles followed. And soon after, a dial tone.

J. T. E.

The History of *Sook's Cookbook*

These receipts, compiled from entries in plantation record books dating as far back as 1836, were given to me shortly before the death of my aunt Sook Faulk in January of 1946. The understanding was that I would share them with Truman Capote, my sister's child, who had been brought up in Sook's hometown, Monroeville, Alabama.

Monroeville is a small town in the Deep South, midway between Montgomery and Mobile. The business section of town was just like those in hundreds of small towns throughout the South, with a courthouse in the middle of the square where old men gathered on a hot day to sit and talk, whittle, and chew tobacco. Mostly they were quiet, but every once in a while one would speak in a slow drawl or shift a squeaky chair. Some tilted chairs back against the courthouse wall and gazed at each other solemnly. When they spoke, the facts were already known, but they figured they might come up with a new answer if they went over the questions one more time.

The houses were big and roomy with opulent gingerbread gothic styling. Great oaks lined the streets, burdened with gray moss hanging from their limbs and gently swaying in the evening breeze. The town boasted of three major churches: the Baptist, the Methodist, and the black church, Mount Zion.

On Saturday afternoon you might hear Uncle Abb Moore, an elderly black man, greet you with his favorite salutation: "You'se well, how's I?" Or you might hear a heated argument about where the word *Dixie* came from. Some old-timers swear that state banks in New Orleans issued ten-dollar notes with the inscription "Ten Dollars" on the face. For fear of insulting their Cajun friends, the descendants of the French Canadians who lived in New Orleans, the reverse side was inscribed "Dix" dollars. They soon became known as Dixies, and the area in which they were used became known as Dixie Land.

Monroeville had none of the legendary fierceness of the South. It had its own simple savagery instead. There were those who remembered the Civil War too well. They were bound together by blood, loneliness, and, most of all, necessity. It was a place of customs and habit.

The sign above the drugstore had been there a long time. The gold had worn off, but you could still read it: Monroe Drugs. The drugstore was a place to go and sit at the wire-legged tables with their matching chairs or up at the counter with the high stools and the cool white marble top. From the counter you could look into the streaked mirror while you drank your lemon or cherry Coke or ate your banana split. It was a place where kids stopped on their way home from school, toting croker sacks holding stiff cats, to read magazines from the stand or just to sit in the cool under the old wooden revolving fan that hung from the high ceiling.

Across the street from the drugstore was Dr. Fripp's general store. It was a heavenly place. He had vegetables, candy, toys, kitchen appliances, crepe paper, horse collars, and just about anything else in the world. Salt mackerel filled wooden barrels. Bins of coffee and pickles in sour-smelling vinegar with flies floating on top surrounded the counter. The old store had never been painted and had aged to a silvery gray. The ceiling was so black above the cross rafters where the horse collars hung that the abundance of spiders was no mystery. One side of the store was covered with tin signs advertising chewing tobacco, chicken feed, soft drinks—primarily Orange Crush and CheerWine, tonics for kidneys, Carter's Little Liver Pills.

All day Dr. Fripp ran back and forth among the cash register, empty crates, and the shelves he was trying to stock. His white hair was always winging back over his ears, giving him the strange look of being about to fly away. He was never able to finish a thing, but this was not entirely his fault. His mind and eyes were permanently brooding and inquisitive as he watched his customers go through his tender lettuce, only to throw it viciously aside, or select a pound of butterbeans, then reject one single bean on the very bottom of the heap.

Heaven knows he tried to be just and charitable, but some of the ladies were as mean as a she-bear with two cubs. It was only natural that he felt a mild hatred for some of his customers and their little torments.

You could walk on around the post office, the old Crook Hotel, and cut up by the mulberry tree, being careful because it dripped worms and leaves all year, to the most prestigious establishment in town, namely, V. H. & C. E. Faulk's Millinery Shop. This pinnacle of shopping in Monroeville was run by Jenny and Callie Faulk. Jenny had a gift for designing hats, and soon the ladies from Mobile, Montgomery, and Birmingham were coming to her shop for their accessories. Eventually her fame spread to Pensacola and New Orleans. She had the ability and the strength to make money and care for her whole family, which included Sook and sometimes Truman.

Corrie Wolff was Jenny's housekeeper and sometime cook; Little Bit was the official cook; and Sem, another cook of unusual talent, was used for all special parties, dinners, weddings, and funerals.

Over Monroeville lay a pattern of good things: church socials, ladies' sewing circles, garden clubs; the picture show; children laughing, running, shouting, licking ice cream cones; weddings with old shoes tied to the newlyweds' car with streamers of white satin blowing in the wind; county fairs bulging with the best cakes and pies.

From this world, I've drawn the best of the food and the fondest of my memories. Most of the receipts come from in and around Monroeville. Some come from towns that no longer exist or that have been renamed. Some come along with comments made by slaves or servants. All capture a world that has already disappeared or is fast doing so.

It's strange, but memories are usually made up of common things, and those things are often tied up with food. A house filled with the smells of good cooking is one of the things all of us remember from our childhoods, from the world we grew up in. Memories of food, all our deepest memories, are like musical phrases in an intricate symphony: they come in modestly, swell to importance, fade into oblivion, and later return, often livelier than they were before.

Truman loved and remembered Sook's Lemon Meringue Pie and had been an active partner in the preparation of her fruitcake, which Truman was to make famous in his story "A Christmas Memory." He did not come to Monroeville for Sook's funeral, but in 1947 he visited me at my home in Dallas, North Carolina, and we started to work on creating a cookbook from the receipts passed on to us by Sook. It was our hope that such a book would evoke memories that many Southerners share with our family, indeed, many people everywhere who love the old ways and the foods and stories that were so much a part of them.

Truman was very eager to have such a cookbook published as a tribute to Sook. He especially wanted her fruitcake receipt and the menu served to Lafayette on his arrival in Claiborne, Alabama, on April 5, 1825, to appear in print, but when Truman skyrocketed to national fame in 1948, the cookbook was pushed aside.

In 1972 Truman came to visit me in Charlotte, North Carolina, and we did extensive work on the project we had begun so long ago. By this time I had written a great deal about the characters in the Faulk household: the cook, Little Bit; Corrie, the housekeeper and some-time cook; Sem Muscadine, another cook; and others.

After that 1972 visit, I continued working on the cookbook, sometimes consulting by telephone with my nephew. The result of our combined efforts is this book, a long overdue tribute to Sook and to the way of life that her receipts embody. It is now also a tribute to Truman, who so loved that life.

RECEIPTS FROM THE

Faulk Household

Sook

Nannie "Sook" Faulk was a charming eccentric whose life revolved around events within the walls of the big white house that belonged to and was dominated by her sister, Jenny.

Sook was a frail little woman with skin drawn taut across her cheekbones, almost translucent, like a fragile teacup held up to the light. She held herself erect, the supple core of her body springing outward to meet life. She moved with a pert, swinging step, her shoulders set and determined.

Her eyes were keen brown, lively, with edges the blue-lavender of seashells. Her hands—large, tender, brown, and gnarled—had an air of magic about them, just like everything else about her. Her smile was the soft, innocent smile of a child. Her baby-soft hair was cropped close to her head, the pink of her skull showing through.

Her favorite dress, a bouquet of printed roses, whispered around the tops of her white tennis shoes. On windy days she stuffed her petticoat into her drawers. When she was flying kites, her face glowed with expectant rapture, burning like a candle inside alabaster.

Born in 1871, six years after the Civil War ended, she learned the value of creating something from nothing. Knowledge about herbs and spices gleaned from the Creek Indians living on the bank of the Alabama River at Claiborne was a mainstay of Sook's experience and was always reflected in her cooking.

Even now I can see clearly the huge kitchen and its window sills filled with herbs and plants. The walls were covered with a list that recorded Sook's "hankerings," month by month. Her pride was another list, this one of the Indian moons, given to her by a chief. It read this way:

January—The Cold Moon
February—The Hunger Moon
March—The Crow Moon
April—The Grass Moon
May—The Planting Moon
June—The Rose Moon
July—The Thunder Moon
August—The Green-Corn Moon
September—The Harvest Moon
October—The Hunting Moon
November—The Frosty Moon
December—The Long-Night Moon

Her herbs and plants sat on snow-white pebbles gathered from the bottom of the Little River. They were a sight to see, the tall, bushy ones in the back, the smaller ones next, and in the front row the dainty, frilly ones. Her pickles and preserves received the same grand treatment in glass-doored cabinets usually reserved for china. Her color index made a rainbow: the reddish-amber mayhaw jelly first, yellow cling peaches brandied in applejack next, then huge red regal strawberries, followed by the pale golden pears with red cherries, and last the dark, rich brown turkey figs.

Little Bit, the cook, was very disturbed over Sook's takeover of the china cabinet, but she was even more disturbed by the plants and herbs because Sook allowed two chameleons to roam amongst them. Regardless of Little Bit's scorn, the two lizards lived happily there, licking drops of water off the foliage with their flicking pink tongues. If you looked carefully, each chameleon had its own favorite plant and could be found curled around the base of its pot, sound asleep, wearing the brown that indicates a relaxed lizard. An agitated chameleon is green, and sometimes Little Bit's anger turned a sleeping lizard green.

There was a practical side to Sook's allowing these lizards to make her plants their home. Chameleons keep herbs free of mealy bugs, red spiders, flies, and almost anything else that would pester a plant. They can become real pets as well and seldom leave once they become accustomed to a home.

Little Bit was never convinced of their virtues, however, and was sometimes heard muttering something along the line of, "Sweet Jesus,

I knowed Mis Nannie had a peck of trouble and brimmin' over, but dem little green devils crawlin' round the pantry makes my backbone fairly crawl."

Sook would be unfazed, saying something like, "Well, it's the Lord's hand."

My favorite memory of Sook is sitting before an early October open fire with her and her big black cat, Joshua, soaking up the warmth. Sook would, after a while, pick Joshua up and settle him in a limp line across her knee, head-on to the fire. His front paws worked at her knee bones with steady prickles, and we were all satisfied that the world was good.

The early mornings were a special time for us. Another memory still comes back to me: standing on the porch with Sook, watching the sky take on the arch of the morning, to curve and cover our little world. Then the sun comes gleaming over the trees, and mockingbirds take breath and sing their morning song.

Sook, like a hard-to-find delicate wildflower, always delighted finders with her rarity, just as her special foods always delighted with their tastes and smells unlike any others in the world.

Sook's Famous "Christmas Memory" Fruitcake

This is the receipt for the fruitcake Truman Capote writes about in "A Christmas Memory," which includes a visit to Mr. Haha Jones, an Indian who operated a "place of sin" down on the banks of the Little River where the whiskey to douse the fruitcakes in was purchased.

A teetotaler herself, Sook nonetheless loved to douse her fruit-cakes with good whiskey. Of course, during Prohibition she had to settle for moonshine corn whiskey, and in reality that meant not Mr. Haha Jones, but Victorio, who claimed to be a full-blooded Apache from New Mexico.

This rather mean-tempered Indian lived in a shack on the banks of the Little River about eight miles from Monroeville. He ran a fish camp and, some people insisted, a whorehouse. We never knew for certain about the latter. He was a huge, gap-toothed man with a sallow complexion. Victorio was ugly, and he was tough. He told us that he was named for the famous Apache guerrilla fighter Victorio, who went on the warpath against the whites in the 1880s and was finally killed in a fight with Mexican troops a few years later.

Victorio's whiskey must have been good because lots of people in the county drank it. He was his own best customer and stayed drunk most of the time.

"Chief Victorio, it is not good for you to drink so much of your whiskey," Sook once cautioned him, using her favorite name for him.

"The white man crazy over tobacco, the Indian crazy over whiskey," was his answer.

Victorio's fish camp/whorehouse was a bad place, all right. Many unpleasant things happened there—fights, knifings, beatings, even an occasional shooting. One time Victorio lost his patience with a rowdy customer and knocked him into a roaring fire. Or so the stories insisted. But his camp was always quiet when we were there.

When the rest of us accompanied Sook on one of her whiskey-buying expeditions, it was, we thought, an adventure fraught with terrible dangers. We always approached Victorio's camp with extreme caution, never knowing what awful atrocities might happen while we were there. Sook, on the other hand, never had the slightest hesitation. Victorio showed great tenderness and regard for Sook and her fruitcakes, and he always gave her a friendly welcome.

"Please, Chief Victorio," Sook would say, after they had made small talk for several minutes, "we would like two quarts of your best whiskey."

Each October Sook would offer to pay him, but Victorio always refused. "Very well, Chief Victorio," Sook would promise, "I will bring you two of my fruitcakes." She would, too. The big Indian loved them. He would pull up a crate and a bottle of his moonshine whiskey and eat big chunks of the cake while slugging away at his bottle.

Everybody knew that Victorio had a wife, but none of us had ever seen her. Truman read somewhere that among the Apaches it was customary to disfigure an erring wife by cutting off her nose. We wondered—did Victorio keep his wife hidden because he had amputated her nose in a fit of drunken jealousy? We never found out.

2 1/2 pounds Brazil nuts
2 1/2 pounds white and dark raisins, mixed

1/2 pound candied cherries

1/2 pound candied pineapple

1 pound citron

1/2 pound blanched almonds

1/2 pound pecan halves

1/2 pound black walnuts

1/2 pound dried figs

1 scant tablespoon nutmeg

1 scant tablespoon cloves

2 tablespoons grated bitter chocolate

1 8-ounce grape jelly

1 8-ounce glass jar grape juice

1 8-ounce glass bourbon whiskey

1 tablespoon cinnamon

1 scant tablespoon allspice

BATTER

2 cups pure butter

2 cups sugar

12 eggs

4 cups flour

The fruitcakes for which Victorio's whiskey was a necessary ingredient were steamed on top of a great black wood stove, then baked in the oven. Any type of steamer that allows the steam to rise may be used.

Cut the fruits and nuts into small pieces and use enough of the flour to dredge them, making a thin coat over all. Cream the butter and sugar, adding one egg at a time, beating well. Add the flour. Add the dredged fruits and nuts, spices, seasoning, and flavorings. Mix thoroughly by hand. Line your cake tin with waxed paper and grease well, then flour. The pan should be large enough to hold a twelve-pound cake.

Pour the mixture into the pan and put it in a steamer over cold water. Close the steamer and bring the water to a rolling boil. After the water boils, lower the heat and steam the cake on top of the stove for about four-and-one-half hours. Preheat the oven to around 250 degrees, and put the cake in and bake it for one hour.

Sook's Buttermilk Biscuits

"Take two and butter them while they're hot" is about as Southern as you can get. When he was young, Sook's biscuits were a favorite after-school snack for Truman.

Sook was happy and lighthearted when she was cooking on the big old black wood stove. That stove would roar, summer or winter, no matter. When questioned about the terrible heat on the hottest days, Sook's stock answer was, "And who cares, pray tell?" It's in answers like this that the webby Southern mind is at its best.

Pulling the golden brown biscuits from the oven, she would glance over at Truman and sing in her stringy voice:

> As green grass grows around the stump,
> I want you for my darling sugar lump!

2 cups plain flour
3/4 teaspoon soda
1/2 teaspoon salt
4 tablespoons pure lard
2/3 cup fresh buttermilk

Preheat the oven to 450 degrees. Sift the dry ingredients—flour, soda, salt—together. Cut in the lard with two forks until the mixture has the appearance of small white gravel. Pour the buttermilk in all at once. Mix gently. Transfer the dough to a floured surface and knead six or seven times. Roll with a floured rolling pin to a half-inch thickness. Cut into the desired size . . . big for a hungry family, smaller if company is coming, and thimble-size for children's tea parties. Bake on a slightly greased baking sheet until the biscuits are a golden brown.

The heart may give the most
useful lessons to the head.

Fresh Lemon Meringue Pie

This was one of Truman's favorite desserts (he also loved the Tiny Fresh Lemon Tarts made by Sem Muscadine). Sook said of this pie, "I make it sour enough to make a pig squeal."

4 tablespoons cornstarch
4 tablespoons flour
2 cups sugar
2 cups boiling water
2 teaspoons pure butter
1/4 teaspoon salt
6 fresh egg yolks
4 grated fresh lemon rinds
3 tablespoons lemon juice
6 egg whites
1 teaspoon cream of tartar
10 tablespoons sugar
1 baked 9-inch pie shell

Preheat the oven to 350 degrees. Mix cornstarch, flour, and sugar; add boiling water, stirring constantly. Cook slowly for about ten minutes. Add the butter, egg yolks, lemon rind, and lemon juice. Cook about five minutes. When the mixture is cool, pour it into a baked pie shell. Beat the egg whites until they are stiff and dry. Add one teaspoon of cream of tartar and sugar into the whites. Spread the meringue on top of the lemon mixture and sprinkle granulated sugar on top of it to make it a nice golden brown. Bake for about fifteen minutes.

Sook's Pulled Cream Mints

2 cups sugar
2/3 cup water
1/4 teaspoon cream of tartar
1 teaspoon cider vinegar
Confectioners' sugar

In a heavy saucepan combine two cups of sugar, two-thirds cup of water, one-quarter teaspoon of cream of tartar, and one teaspoon of cider vinegar. Bring this to a rapid boil. Do not stir. Wash down the sides of the saucepan from time to time with a brush dipped in water. Boil until the syrup reaches a hard ball stage (260 degrees on a candy thermometer). You can test the syrup's readiness by dropping a small amount into a cold glass of water.

Remove the syrup, and as soon as it stops boiling, pour it onto an oiled marble slab. Wait a few minutes, then begin turning the edges into the center. Let it stand until it is cool enough to handle.

Sprinkle the candy with three-quarters teaspoon of oil of peppermint and a few drops of green coloring. Dip your fingers into cornstarch, and pull the candy until it is lukewarm and difficult to stretch. Do not wait too long. Pull it into a long rope about one-half inch in diameter, and cut the rope with scissors into small pieces.

Drop the mints into sifted confectioners' sugar, cover, and let them stand overnight to ripen. The next day, shake the sugar from the mints and store them in a tightly covered jar for several days before eating.

Sook's Famous "Milk Flowers"

> Made in the shade, sold in the sun,
> If you haven't got a nickel, you can't get none.

In the hot summertime when appetites are dulled and nothing seems right, it's ice cream weather. For Sook, ice cream was something magical that she named milk flowers.

There was a ritual surrounding the first ice cream of the season. Almost miraculously, the ice cream freezer would appear in the front yard under the biggest shade tree. The gears would be checked, the metal can and dasher would be washed and scalded, and the wooden tub would be inspected for damages.

While the custard for the ice cream cooled, a couple of small fry would head to the ice house for a dime's worth of ice. They took a strong broom handle with them for carrying their purchase home. After he had chipped the ice, the long, lanky black man who waited on customers would tie a brown jute string around it, and the children would slip the stick under his knot, each holding an end of the broom stick with the ice between them. Carrying this odd bundle, they would hurry home. The highlight of going to the ice house was the privilege of going into the cold, inky darkness while the ice was being chipped from the huge block, always watching the heavy door for a dreadful (yet delightful) feeling of being locked in.

Nothing can touch the old-fashioned hand freezer for making ice cream. The sound of the turning crank and the crunch of the ice and rock salt against the tub excites the appetite to a new pitch of expectation. Homemade ice cream never wholly loses the magic of its spell. Like most first loves, nothing can ever take its place.

Ice cream is as American as the *Mayflower* Pilgrims.

Burnt Sugar Ice Cream

2 cups sugar
6 whole eggs, slightly beaten
1 1/2 cups sugar
One pinch salt
2 quarts cream, one half-whipped
Pure vanilla extract, to taste

Caramelize two cups of granulated sugar in a heavy iron pot and let it boil until it is a good brown. Combine in the top of a double boiler the beaten eggs, one cup of sugar, the salt, and the first quart of cream (unwhipped). After the custard has thickened, add the caramelized sugar while it is very hot. Strain and cool.

Add the vanilla and the extra quart of half-whipped cream. Freeze in an old-fashioned hand freezer. When the ice is chipped fine and layered with coarse salt around the metal cylinder, it's time to start turning the handle to freeze the custard. Always place a clean cloth around the neck of the freezer to prevent the salt from getting in the ice cream.

When the crank gets hard to turn, you hear, "It's ready!"

Remove the handle from the cylinder and drain the briny water through the bunghole. Carefully wipe the top with a clean towel and take it off. Let the ice cream sit for about ten minutes to mellow.

Then lift the dasher, filled with frozen jewels clinging to its blade, from the churn. Being allowed to lick this tasty treasure is one of childhood's fondest memories.

Sook's Brown Turkey Fig Ice Cream

When the rich honey oozes from tiny rifts in the blue and brown and purple skin, it's time to make fig ice cream. When Truman came to spend summers in Monroeville, this was one of his favorites.

1/2 cup milk
2 egg yolks
1/2 cup cream, whipped
1 quart ripe figs
1 tablespoon lemon juice
1/2 cup sugar
One teaspoon vanilla extract

Scald one-half cup of milk and slowly stir in two well-beaten egg yolks. Cook the mixture over boiling water, stirring constantly, until the custard coats a silver spoon. Cool and fold the custard into one-half cup of cream, whipped. Peel one quart of ripe figs (the juice should be running out the top) and press them through a sieve. Sprinkle the mashed figs with one tablespoon lemon juice, stir in one-half cup of sugar and one teaspoon of pure vanilla, and add this mixture to the custard. Blend the ingredients thoroughly and hand freeze.

Fresh Peach Ice Cream

2 well-beaten eggs
1 cup sugar
1 cup light corn syrup
2 cups milk
2 cups cream
1/4 cup lemon juice
2 cups mashed very ripe peaches, sweetened

Add the sugar to the eggs gradually while beating them. Stir in the corn syrup, milk, cream, and lemon juice. Mix well. Add the peaches and start freezing, being careful not to stop churning or the ice cream will be lumpy.

Sook's Persimmon Cake

The following was written in the margin next to this receipt:

Raccoon up the 'simmon tree
Possum on the ground.
Raccoon shake them 'simmons down,
Possum pass 'em round.

2 1/2 cups brown sugar
2/3 cup butter
3 whole eggs
2 1/2 cups flour
2 teaspoons cinnamon
2 teaspoons allspice
2 cups persimmon pulp
2 cups raisins
2 cups chopped pecans

Preheat the oven to 250 degrees. Cream the sugar and butter; add the eggs. Beat well. Sift all dry ingredients and add them to the sugar and shortening. Add the persimmons. Then put in the raisins and pecans. Back in a tube pan for about two hours.

Sook's Popovers

7/8 cup fresh sweet milk
1 cup flour, sifted and measured
1 teaspoon salt
2 eggs

Preheat the oven to 450 degrees. Beat the eggs together until they are light; add the salt and half of the milk. Mix into a smooth batter, free of any lumps. Add the remainder of the milk, which produces a very thin batter.

Grease the popover pans and have them hot. Fill each cup half full or less. Place the pans in the center of a hot oven. Cook at 450 degrees for fifteen minutes, then reduce the heat and continue baking at 325 degrees until the popovers are dry and crisp.

Do not open the oven for the first ten minutes. When the pastries are well popped, lower the heat to make them crisp and dry them out. The popovers will be hollow inside, almost like a bubble.

Note: There is no grease or leavening in real popovers. They must be made with sweet milk.

Six O'Clock Rolls

2 yeast cakes or packages dry yeast
2 eggs
2 teaspoons salt
1 cup mashed Irish potatoes
Flour to make medium dough
1 cup scalded milk
1/2 cup sugar
1/2 cup lukewarm water
2/3 cup butter

Put the mashed potatoes in a bowl; add the shortening, sugar, salt, and scalded milk. When this mixture is tepid, add the yeast, which you have dissolved in the lukewarm water. Now add just enough flour to make a medium-stiff dough.

Put this mixture in the refrigerator to rise gradually until you are ready to make the rolls. When they are made out at four o'clock, they are ready for a six o'clock dinner. Make the dough itself up at about nine o'clock in the morning.

Preheat the oven to 400 degrees. When the oven is ready, cook the rolls for eighteen to twenty minutes.

The crust of these rolls is wonderfully tender.

You will go hungry within the month
if you take bread while you still
have some on your plate.

Old-Fashioned Pulled Candy

Whenever Sook got the green melancholia, she made candy.

3 cups sugar
1/4 cup vinegar
2 tablespoons butter
1/2 cup water

Mix and cook slowly these ingredients until test drops are brittle when dropped in a cup of cold water. Do not stir while cooking. Pour out on a cold, buttered marble slab. When the candy is cool enough to handle, butter your whole hand, take up part of the candy, and pull it with long, firm strokes until it becomes porous and light in color. Let the ropes of pulled candy sit on the buttered slab until they become cool and hard. Cut the candy into bite-sized pieces. Food coloring may be added for special occasions, and adding a drop of pure oil of mint makes delicious mints.

Divinity

2 cups sugar
1/2 cup water
1/3 cup light corn syrup
2 egg whites
1/2 teaspoon pure vanilla
1 1/2 cups chopped pecans

Combine the sugar, water, and corn syrup in a heavy two-quart sauce-pan and bring the mixture to a boil over a high heat, stirring the sugar until it is dissolved. Then cook briskly, uncovered, for ten to fifteen minutes, until the syrup reaches a temperature of 225 degrees on a candy thermometer or until a drop spooned into ice water immediately forms a brittle ball.

In a deep bowl, beat the egg whites with a wire whisk until they are stiff enough to stand in unwavering peaks on the whisk when it is lifted from the bowl.

As soon as the syrup reaches the proper temperature, remove the pan from the heat. Whipping the egg whites constantly with the whisk, pour in the syrup in a very slow, thin stream. (Do not scrape the saucepan; the syrup that clings to it is likely to have gone to sugar.)

Add the vanilla and continue to beat for about ten minutes longer, or until the candy begins to lose its gloss and is thick enough to hold its shape almost solidly in a spoon. Stir in the pecans at once.

Without waiting a second, drop the divinity by the tablespoon onto waxed paper, letting each spoonful mound slightly in the center (make a peak). Place a whole half pecan on top of each piece. Allow the candy to sit undisturbed until it is firm. (When divinity was served at weddings, it was customary to place a whole cherry on top.)

Jenny

Jenny, matriarch of the Fault family, was born in 1873, a child of a lost war, who grew up knowing what a life of deprivation meant. As an adult, she became the dominant character in the Faulk household and assumed responsibility for the entire family, including her sister Callie and her brother Bud.

Jenny was a beautiful woman with hair the color of red oak leaves in autumn. Her hands were strong and squarish with faint freckles, like a pear ready to pick. Her skin was translucent in its dazzling whiteness, with ropes of pearls glowing coolly against her skin. She was born as stylish as a tomcat with white paws and waistcoat.

She never cared much for children but always provided well for them. Neither did she care for the running of the household. Jenny seemed to have that quality you sometimes see in old gray foxes and grizzled rats: the capacity to survive. After her hard life and long-awaited success, she wanted only the finer things in life: teas, clothes, and travel.

The only conversation the children of the household had with Jenny took place when she was disgusted about something. Then she would say, "If you don't behave yourselves, I will skin you like a catfish." She was the type of woman everyone looked up to, and she attracted men like flies around a watermelon cutting.

One of Jenny's favorite social occasions was the ritual of the afternoon tea. Anna, Britain's Duchess of Bedford, is said to have originated the afternoon tea in 1840. She claimed it was a way to alleviate her "fainting spells" caused by dinner's not being served in fashionable homes until around 8:00 P.M. Tea started out with tidbits but worked up to groaning boards loaded with cakes, jellies, meringues, and meat sandwiches.

In the South, tea was usually served around four in the afternoon. It was opulent and extravagant, almost to the point of vulgarity. The ritual provided the very wealthy and the middle class an enjoyable way of passing—or wasting—time as they entertained each other.

Jenny had an elegant Georgian tea table that she covered with a fine lace tablecloth and set with dainty Dresden tea cups and saucers, each on a tea plate with an organdy tea napkin between the plate and the saucer. The handsome silver galleried tea tray was the resting place for an elegant silver tea kettle with a spirit burner, a sugar basket with its blue Bristol glass liner, a helmet-shaped creamer, a strainer, a hot water jug, and the impressive "slop" bowl into which the dregs from each guest's cup were poured before the cup was refilled.

When Jenny entertained someone very special, she would have the tea sandwiches made into little bunches (one of each kind) and tied with ribbon bows. The guests could then simply lift out the tiny bundles and place them on their plates.

After the guests departed, it was customary for the mistress of the house to have a servant bring two bowls of hot water, one soapy, the other clear for rinsing, and a fine linen towel for drying. Jenny washed the cups and saucers herself. China and porcelain of this fine quality were too valuable to allow the servants to handle.

Jenny always purchased her teas from Mobile or New Orleans. Her favorite was Darjeeling, which was supposed to be the finest tea in all the world. It grows high in the mountains near Nepal and tastes like black currants. Another tea she liked was Lapsang Souchong from China. It has a large leaf and is hearty, smoky, and rich in flavor. For ordinary family gatherings, she used a black tea.

The secret to good tea is to bring the kettle to the teapot, having let the water come to a boil but not boil more than a second. Every second it bubbles, oxygen is being carried away, and overboiled water makes the tea taste muddy.

Let the tea steep for about five minutes, although some teas, such as Jenny's Lapsang Souchong, take longer. Avoid aluminum or worn enamel on metal for brewing tea as it will taint the flavor. A porcelain pot is best for all types of tea. If you are using loose tea, the general rule is one teaspoon for each person and one for the pot.

Jenny's Tiny Cream Puffs

1/2 cup pure butter
1 cup boiling water
1 cup regular flour
1/4 teaspoon salt
4 fresh eggs

Preheat the oven to 350 degrees. Melt the butter in water. Add the flour and salt together and stir vigorously. Cook, stirring constantly, until the mixture forms a ball that does not separate. Remove from the heat and cool slightly.

Add the eggs, one at a time, beating vigorously after each addition, until the mixture is smooth. Drop from a teaspoon one inch apart onto a greased cooking pan. Bake in a very hot oven for fifteen minutes, then in a slower oven (325 degrees) for twenty-five minutes.

Remove to a rack. When they are completely cool, cut off the tops and fill each puff with old-fashioned chicken salad. This receipt will make about three dozen puffs.

Old-Fashioned Chicken Salad

3 cups cooked chicken, diced
1 1/2 cups celery, diced
1 teaspoon salt
3 hard-cooked eggs, quartered
3 sweet pickles, chopped fine
Dash white pepper
Mayonnaise to bind
1/2 tablespoon fresh chives
1 tablespoon fresh parsley, chopped

Mix ingredients together, chill, and then spoon into tiny cream puffs to make sandwiches.

Jenny's Honey-Walnut Tea Bread

Children in the South and probably elsewhere all ask the question: "How does a bee make honey?"

Here's how. A girl bee makes honey in a special stomach. First, she goes to a flower for the same reason that we go to the grocery store. This is where the makings are.

The girl bee sips the sweet flour juice, called nectar, up through her mouth, which is shaped like a tiny soda straw, down into her honey stomach, where it becomes the most healthful kind of sweet a person or a bee could ever want.

She wings back to the hive to feed the baby bees a delicious treat called bee bread. It is made out of honey mixed with flower pollen. The honey that is left goes into the honeycomb. The bee then seals the comb with wax, which she also makes herself.

That's how honey is made.

    12 tablespoons melted butter
    1 1/3 cups pure honey
    1/2 cup milk
    2 fresh eggs
    2 1/2 tablespoons fresh lemon juice
    1/4 teaspoon baking powder
    1 teaspoon ground cloves
    1/4 teaspoon salt
    1 cup walnuts, chopped fine
    1/2 cup diced candied orange peel

Preheat the oven to 325 degrees. Using a wooden spoon, combine the honey, eggs, butter, milk, and lemon juice in a large bowl until the ingredients are well mixed. In a separate bowl, mix together the flour, baking powder, salt, and cloves. Add the flour mixture to the honey mixture and beat until light. Mix in the walnuts and orange peel and pour into well-greased loaf pans. Bake for one hour or until a broom straw comes out clean. This receipt will make two loaves.

Jenny's Lace Cookies

3 tablespoons butter, softened
1 cup brown sugar
1 egg, well beaten
4 tablespoons flour
1 cup ground almonds, blanched
1 teaspoon pure brandy
1 teaspoon pure vanilla

Preheat the oven to 350 degrees. Butter your cookie sheets well. Cream the brown sugar and butter, then blend in the flour, eggs, vanilla, ground almonds, and brandy. Add the brandy last. Drop the batter by half-teaspoons onto a buttered cookie sheet, spacing them well apart. Bake for about eight to ten minutes. The cookies will be crisp and lacy. Remove them quickly from the oven and cool them on a wire rack. This receipt makes about three dozen cookies.

Jenny's Tea Sugar Cookies

This receipt is an old Southern favorite.

2 cups sugar
2 fresh eggs
2 teaspoons water
1 teaspoon soda
1 cup buttermilk
1 cup pure butter, melted
3 teaspoons pure vanilla extract
1/2 teaspoon salt

1 teaspoon baking powder

6 cups all-purpose flour (approximately)

Beat the sugar and eggs together well. Dissolve the soda in the water and add to the sugar mixture, along with the butter, buttermilk, and vanilla. Beat well. Stir in the baking powder and salt; gradually stir in flour. Cover and chill for at least one hour.

Preheat the oven to 400 degrees. Shape the dough into small balls. Put them on a greased baking sheet. Flatten each ball with a fork dipped in extra sugar. Bake until they are a delicate brown. This receipt usually makes around six dozen cookies.

Fresh Blueberry Tea Bread

2 cups flour

1 cup sugar

1 1/2 cups fresh blueberries

2 eggs

1 cup top milk

3 tablespoons butter, melted

1 teaspoon fresh orange rind, grated

Preheat the oven to 350 degrees. After washing the blueberries, dry them off very well with a linen towel.

Mix the flour and sugar. Stir in the blueberries. In a separate bowl beat together the eggs, milk, butter, and orange rind. Add this mixture, all at once, to the flour mixture. Stir until all ingredients are damp. Turn into a greased loaf pan. Bake for about an hour or until a broom straw comes out clean. After the bread is cool, cut it into squares and sprinkle each square with finely pounded sugar.

Jenny's White Crabmeat Tea Sandwiches

1 1/2 cups white crabmeat, finely chopped

4 hard-boiled egg yolks, sieved

Mayonnaise to bind

4 fresh scallions, finely chopped

Salt and freshly ground white pepper to taste
Juice of one lemon
Lemon-and-Parsley Butter

Mix all the ingredients together. Spread ten to twelve slices of bread with Lemon-and-Parsley Butter, then with the filling. Top with a second slice of bread. Remove the crusts and cut in any shape desired.

Fresh Lemon-and-Parsley Butter

2 cups sweet butter, softened
1 teaspoon salt
Sprinkling of freshly ground white pepper
Finely grated rind and juice of one lemon
1 cup fresh parsley, chopped

Make a paste of all the ingredients and add parsley.

Creamed Butter for Tea Sandwiches

1 1/2 cups sweet butter, softened
2 tablespoons heavy cream
Pinch of mild French mustard
Juice of 1/2 lemon
Salt and pepper

Blend all ingredients to a soft, spreadable consistency.

Fresh Chive Butter

2 cups sweet butter, softened
1 teaspoon fresh lemon juice
Freshly ground white pepper to taste
1/2 cup chives, finely snipped

Blend the butter with the lemon juice and pepper. Mix in the snipped chives. This butter may be stored in the freezer if it is properly packaged.

Fresh Mint Butter

2 cups sweet butter, softened
1 cup fresh mint leaves, packed
2 teaspoons fresh lemon juice
1 teaspoon salt
1 teaspoon sugar

Thoroughly mash all the ingredients. Rub through a fine-meshed sieve. Pack and store in the freezer, if desired.

The 1890 Victorian Cucumber Tea Sandwich

Cool and refreshing, cucumber sandwiches are one of the most delicious of all tea sandwiches, but they are messy because the insides have a tendency to slither out.

1 fresh cucumber (12 inches)
1 tablespoon virgin olive oil
Scant teaspoon sugar
1 tablespoon lemon juice
Freshly ground white pepper
Salt to taste

Cut the cucumber into slices as thin as possible. Very lightly salt the slices and leave them to drain in a colander, lightly weighing them down with a plate, for at least two hours. Press them from time to time to get rid of excess juices.

Combine the sliced and drained cucumbers with the oil, lemon juice, sugar, and a sprinkling of white pepper. Spread thin slices of day-old bread with creamed butter and fill in the sandwich.

Jenny's Fresh Raspberry Shortcake

2 cups all-purpose flour
1/4 cup granulated sugar
Pinch salt

1 tablespoon baking powder
8 tablespoons fresh butter
1 fresh egg
1/2 cup milk

RASPBERRY FILLING

2 pints heavy cream, whipped
1 tablespoon finely powdered sugar
1 teaspoon pure vanilla extract
1 pint fresh raspberries

Wash berries and drain well. Flavor the whipped cream with the vanilla and sugar.

Preheat the oven to 400 degrees. Grease thoroughly an eight-inch round cake tin. In a bowl combine the flour, sugar, baking powder, and salt. Cut the butter into the flour mixture until it resembles coarse meal. Mix the egg and the milk. Make a well in the center of the flour-butter mixture and pour the liquid ingredients into the well. Stir but do not overbeat. There may be a few lumps.

Put the dough in the pan and be sure it is evenly distributed. Bake for twenty-five minutes. To remove, gently loosen the edges of the shortcake with a knife. Turn the shortcake onto a rack to cool.

When it is cool, cut the cake in half to produce two layers. Cover the bottom layer with the flavored whipped cream. Then over the whipped cream add a generous layer of fresh raspberries. Place the top half of the shortcake over the raspberries and cream and spread it with the remaining whipped cream. Sprinkle the top with a few raspberries.

Ripe raspberries have a subtle flavor, an exquisite bouquet, and a silky texture that make them ambrosial, whether served with a dusting of fine sugar, with a heavy cream, or with a touch of Madeira. Do not use kirsch or framboise with fresh raspberries as they are too harsh and will overshadow their delicacy.

Jenny's Devil Cake

This cake is delicious if left for a few days before cutting. After it ages a bit, it can be sliced very thin.

    1/2 cup sweet butter
    1 1/4 cups sugar
    2 eggs
    6 tablespoons cocoa
    2 cups sifted flour
    1 teaspoon baking powder
    1 teaspoon salt
    1 cup sour cream
    1 teaspoon baking soda
    1 teaspoon pure vanilla

Preheat the oven to 350 degrees. Grease and flour two nine-inch layer-cake pans. Cream together the butter and sugar; add the eggs, one at a time, beating after each addition. Sift together cocoa, baking powder, flour, and salt. Mix the sour cream with the baking soda. Alternately add the cocoa mixture and the sour cream mixture to the butter mixture. Add the vanilla. Bake for thirty to forty minutes. Cool.

FROSTING
    1 1/2 cups sugar
    1/2 cup water
    1 1/2 teaspoon vinegar
    3 egg whites
    1/8 teaspoon salt
    1 teaspoon vanilla
    2 tablespoons cocoa

Boil the sugar, water, and vinegar to 238 degrees or until the syrup spins a long thread when dropped from the tip of a spoon. Beat the egg whites until they are stiff, then gradually add the syrup, beating constantly until the frosting holds its shape. Add the salt and vanilla. Fold in the cocoa just before spreading the frosting between the layers and on the top and the sides of the cake.

Orange Pecan Cake

3/4 cup sugar
3/4 cup sweet butter, softened
1 egg
1 cup all-purpose flour
1/2 teaspoon salt
1/2 teaspoon baking soda
1/2 cup buttermilk
Grated rind of 1 orange
1/3 cup chopped dates
1/2 cup pecan pieces

Preheat the oven to 350 degrees. Lightly grease a tube cake pan. Cream together the butter and one-half cup of sugar until light. Add the egg and beat until the mixture is fluffy. Sift together the flour, baking powder, baking soda, and salt. Alternately add the flour mixture and the buttermilk to the butter and egg mixture. Add the grated orange rind and fold in the dates and nuts, to which two tablespoons of flour have been added. Bake for about fifty minutes.

GLAZE FOR THE CAKE

1/3 cup fresh orange juice
2 tablespoons orange liqueur
Confectioners' sugar
1/4 cup granulated sugar

Mix the orange juice, liqueur, and granulated sugar. While the cake is hot, prick the top with the tines of a fork and slowly pour the orange mixture over it. Let it cool in the pan. Wrap the cake or cover it in the pan and let it sit for two or three days. When you are ready to serve it, sprinkle the top with confectioners' sugar.

Bud's Catfish Stew

Just as Jenny dominated the household, she dominated the kitchen. Still, Bud and Callie had their specialties.

6 slices lean bacon
1 1/2 cups onion, finely chopped
6 or 7 medium-sized fresh tomatoes
2 large boiling potatoes, peeled and cut into 1-inch pieces
1 pound catfish trimmings (head, tail, and bones)
2 tablespoons Worcestershire sauce
1 teaspoon Tabasco
2 teaspoons salt
Sprinkle of freshly ground white pepper
2 pounds catfish fillets, cut into 1 1/2 inch pieces
1/2 clove fresh garlic

In a heavy frying pan, fry the bacon over a moderate heat until it is crisp and brown and all the fat has been rendered. Drain on a paper towel, then crumble the bacon into small bits and set aside. Add the onions and garlic to the remaining fat, stirring frequently. Cook for about five minutes. Stir in the tomatoes, potatoes, catfish trimmings, Worcestershire, Tabasco, salt, and a few grindings of white pepper and bring to a boil over a high heat. Reduce the heat to low, cover tightly, and simmer for thirty minutes.

Remove the catfish trimmings and discard them. Add the catfish fillets and the reserved bacon and mix well. Cover and simmer over a low heat for ten minutes or until the fish flakes easily when prodded with the tines of a fork.

Bud's Mint Julep

Spearmint and peppermint are two of the most popular members of the large mint family. Peppermint is the one responsible for that treacherous Southern specialty the mint julep.

Men in the South refer to this as "the most delectable libation of man." It has been known to get you stiff as a cow's ear. A famous old

Alabama verse about Southern men and their mint juleps goes this way:

> Alabama, oh my Alabama,
> Where the corn is full of kernels
> And the Colonel's full of corn!

Get a silver goblet and put about one tablespoon of cold water in it. Then add sugar until the mixture gets silvery and thick as oil.

Crush fresh mint with the back of a silver spoon and carefully cover every section of the goblet and all around the border with the crushed mint. Leave no surface untouched. Throw the remaining mint away.

In a fresh linen towel, dry crushed ice to get the moisture out. Doing this allows the goblet to frost on the outside. Fill the goblet with crushed ice, then pour bourbon over the ice. Let it trickle slowly through the ice, then sit for a moment. Top it with a fresh sprig of mint that is perfect and entirely without bruise marks.

Callie's Bride's Biscuits

Callie was a rare and elegant lady, like a piece of fine point lace. Her hand had known no harder work than delicate embroidery, and her mind never wandered beyond her own surroundings.

She was the kind of Southern lady who was taught from birth to give the impression when she walked that the ground was hardly worthy for her to tread.

As children, we were never allowed to lean back in a good chair or loll on the sofa. These rules were to keep us from "going bad."

After one of her lectures, Callie would give us a sidelong glance that seemed to say, "Aren't you glad you're who you are?"

Being a schoolteacher, she was full of advice. Her favorite for Truman was: "You don't want to grow up and suffer from mental malnutrition, do you?" To the older children she said, "Children today are going to hell by the wagonload."

1/2 cup butter, softened
1 cup flour
1 three-ounce package cream cheese, softened

Preheat the oven to 350 degrees. Blend together the butter and cheese. Mix in the flour and knead to make a dough. Roll out on a floured board and cut with a very small biscuit cutter. Bake until the biscuits are brown and puffy, about fifteen minutes.

Rock an empty cradle, and
you will be an old maid.

Aunt Pallie

Stories retold about the South through a hundred years or more are embellished in the telling and become more legend than fact. But it is a fact that every Southern home of any consequence had its "Mammy." No picture of the South would be complete without this central character who ruled the lives of her white family.

Aunt Pallie (she vowed she was named for the goddess of wisdom, Pallas Athene) was one of those women. She, like all the others, had her little cabin at the rear of the big house where the children gathered to sneak inside to eat and sit on the sweet-smelling corn-shuck bed. There was always a fire in the limestone fireplace in Aunt Pallie's cabin, no matter what the season.

When there was an expectant mother in her care, Aunt Pallie would talk about "my baby" before and after the birth. She watched the cravings of the mother very carefully to make sure that the mother didn't eat anything that would hurt her baby.

She blamed long noses on the mother's having visited the circus or looking too long at an anteater. After the child's birth, she disregarded the instructions of the doctor and took her own "precautions." One was requiring the mother to empty out the ashes from Aunt Pallie's burning of the afterbirth so that the mother's renewed strength would be ensured.

Aunt Pallie flatly refused to sweep under the bed of the mother and the new child because she was afraid doing so would mean that they would never leave the bed. She paid no attention to the orders for boiled water for the baby. When she had a chance, she slipped down to the woods to a fresh spring and carried the baby its first taste of water in the mother's silver thimble.

She brushed the baby's feet with stiff bristles of a broom, saying, "If I didn't sweep off his feet, no tellin' how old he'd be 'fore he walked." Holding a baby near a mirror so that he could see himself was almost fatal in her mind—doing so was responsible for every illness that might strike the child thereafter.

Aunt Pallie's babies had a taste of everything from the mother's table. They had tea for colic and a good rubbing, including the top of the head, for colds. If she could get away with it, Aunt Pallie tied a bag of sassafras around their necks for protection. When the child grew older and enjoyed perfect health, she declared it was because she had not once failed to hang his undershirts up by the sleeves when she washed them.

When Aunt Pallie was peeved with a mother, she complained, "I had ten chillun and was up washin' the didies when they was three days old. Trouble with white folks is, they overlooks the mos' important things. You has to take precautions."

A Mammy's Wit and Wisdom

Never shut your mouth with a snap. The corners will turn down.

Always keep your head up and your dress down.

If you can grab God's shirt-tail, you can be pulled through anything.

I've told you once, I've told you twice: Don't be a mother before you're a wife.

A morning rain is like an old woman's dance; it's soon over.

If you sing before you eat, You'll cry before you sleep.

Thorns do not prick unless you lean against them.

Little Bit

Little Bit was the main cook in the Faulk household. She was a huge woman with the agility of a Siamese cat. Her background was part Indian, part Negro, and part Cajun.

She had a deep scar running across her left cheek from the tip of her ear to her chin. But it didn't detract from her oval cameo of a face or her long coal-black hair parted in the middle and combed over her temples. For so slender a face, her mouth was startlingly full and red-lipped.

Little Bit's love for men was no secret. She loved to talk about her love life, and at the drop of a hat she would say, "There's no sweeter place to lay for love than in a fresh haymow. Gawd, just smellin' that mixture of horse and hay is purely like bitin' into unexpected pepper."

One of Little Bit's favorite sayings was, "Black-eyed people are inclined to evil; green-eyed, to be sharp and cunning; blue-eyed, kind and honest; and brown-eyed, gentle and innocent."

When it came to cooking, Little Bit had no equal.

It is better to be laughed at
for not being married
than to be unable to laugh
because you are.

Cajun Rice from Louisiana

1 pound ground beef
1 pound fresh ground pork
1/2 cup oil
1/2 cup flour
3/4 pound fresh ground pork livers
1 bell pepper, chopped
3 stalks celery, chopped
3 onions, chopped
1 1/2 cups water
Pepper, salt, and cayenne to taste
3/4 cup fresh minced parsley
3 cups cooked rice
1/2 cup green onion tops, chopped

Mix the oil and flour to make a light brown roux. Sauté the beef, liver, and pork in a separate pot until they are light brown; add the bell pepper, onion, and celery. Cook until the onions are transparent. Add the roux and water to the meat mixture and simmer about forty-five minutes. Add the black pepper, salt, and cayenne pepper, green onion tops, and parsley. Mix well.

When you are ready to serve the dish, mix the meat mixture with the rice. This will serve about eight people.

Cajun Banana Fritters

1 1/4 cups sifted flour
1 1/4 teaspoon salt
2 teaspoons baking powder
1 1/4 tablespoon sugar
1 egg, beaten
1/3 cup milk
3 or 4 bananas, ripe, peeled, and cut into 3–4 diagonal pieces
Oil for frying
Pounded sugar

Sift one cup of flour, baking powder, salt, and sugar together. Combine the eggs, milk, and melted butter and add them to the dry ingredients. Mix until the batter is smooth. This will make a stiff batter, which makes a fritter that remains crisp for a good while after it is fried.

Roll the banana pieces in the remaining quarter-cup of flour. Dip them into the fritter batter, completely coating each piece. Fry in the oil, heated to 375 degrees, turning until the fritters brown on all sides. Drain them on a towel and sprinkle with the pounded sugar while they are hot.

Little Bit's Barbecue Sauce

Little Bit had great pride and conviction about the mixing of her barbeque sauce. It was as hot as the distilled essence of red peppers could make it, but sour and sweet underneath—an experience mixed equally with torture and delight.

3/4 cup onion, finely chopped
2 ribs fresh celery, chopped
1 clove garlic, minced
1 fresh red pepper, chopped
1 fresh green pepper, chopped
3 tablespoons dry mustard
2 tablespoons salt
1/3 cup pure olive oil
3/4 cup ketchup
3/4 cup water
1/3 cup vinegar
3 tablespoons brown sugar
1/2 teaspoon Tabasco sauce
Freshly ground black pepper

Preheat the oven to 350 degrees. In a heavy iron pot, cook the onions, celery, garlic, red pepper, and green pepper in olive oil until tender. Add the other ingredients and simmer for one hour. Pour over whatever meat you choose and bake covered in the oven for another hour. Uncover and cook for an additional thirty minutes.

Barbecued Spareribs

1 cup onions, finely chopped
1 cup freshly made ketchup (receipt follows)
1 cup peach preserves
1/4 cup dark brown sugar
1/4 cup distilled white vinegar
1/4 cup Worcestershire sauce
1 teaspoon dry mustard
1/4 teaspoon Tabasco
1/2 teaspoon basil
1/2 teaspoon thyme
1 clove garlic, chopped
4 1/2 pound spareribs
2 teaspoons salt
Fresh ground black pepper
2 lemons, cut into 1/4-inch strips

While the oven is being heated to 400 degrees, prepare the barbecue basting sauce. Combine the onions, thyme, basil, garlic, ketchup, peach preserves, brown sugar, vinegar, Worcestershire sauce, and mustard in a saucepan. Stir constantly with a wooden spoon while bringing the mixture to a boil. Reduce the heat to low and simmer for four or five minutes.

Arrange the spareribs, flesh side up, side by side on a rack in a large shallow roasting pan. Sprinkle them with the salt and a few grindings of pepper. Brush the ribs with the sauce and lay the sliced lemons on top. Bake uncovered in the middle of the oven for one-and-a-half hours. The ribs are done if the meat shows no resistance when pierced deeply with the point of a sharp knife.

Fresh Tomato Ketchup

Most likely tomatoes originated in what is now Peru and Ecuador. They were taken back to Europe along with gold and silver and grown on the continent as a pretty curiosity. The French gave them the name *pomme d'amour*, "love apples," and the Italians called them *pomodori*, "golden apples." Most scholars think both words were derived from *pomo di Mori,* Italian for "Moorish apple," in reference to their Spanish background.

Tomato ketchup is always made in large quantities during the fresh tomato season. It is a mainstay during the winter months.

1 peck fresh tomatoes, peeled
6 tablespoons salt
1 teaspoon red pepper
6 tablespoons ground mustard
2 tablespoons celery seed
2 teaspoons ground mace
1 quart vinegar
10 large onions, chopped
4 tablespoons black pepper
2 teaspoons ground cloves
5 tablespoons mustard seed
1/2 pound horseradish
2 teaspoons cinnamon
1 1/2 pounds white sugar

Cook all the spices with the tomatoes and onions until the tomatoes are soft. Strain through a sieve and add vinegar and sugar. Cook until thick. Cooking may take anywhere from five to six hours. This will make about seven or eight pints of ketchup. Pack in sterile jars. Seal.

Little Bit's Cajun Fresh Shrimp

Ingredients for Cajun, or Acadian, cooking are borrowed from classic French cuisine, then combined with elements of classic Spanish cooking. Herbs and spices common in Spain and France blend with spices and seasoning techniques learned from the Chickasaws and Choctaws. To this international scene the exotic tastes and magic seasonings of Africa also make a contribution, and the result is the root of all Cajun cooking.

This cuisine, unlike Creole cooking, uses herbs, seasonings, and spices to bring out the full flavor of the main ingredient. The result is not highly seasoned, and the original flavor of that main ingredient predominates. There is a French saying that perfectly describes

Cajun cooking: "L'excès en tout est défaut." It translates, "Excess in everything is a fault."

    2 pounds fresh butter
    1 teaspoon rosemary, freshly ground
    3 tablespoons black pepper, freshly ground
    1 teaspoon Tabasco
    4 sliced fresh lemons
    4 teaspoons salt
    3 cloves garlic, mashed
    10 pounds fresh large shrimp, unpeeled, heads on

Preheat the oven to 400 degrees. Melt the butter in a heavy saucepan. Add the pepper, rosemary, hot sauce, salt, garlic, and lemons. Mix well. Place the shrimp in a large shallow pan and pour the sauce over them. Stir well until all the shrimp are coated. Bake for about twenty minutes, turning once. The shells will be pink and the meat white.

Cajun Roux

He who goes slowly, goes surely.

Many Cajun dishes require a roux. Most Acadian cooks say a successful roux is made by slowly sprinkling flour in melted shortening to brown slowly while you stir it constantly. The secret is to add cold water or stock, spices, and herbs gradually. True Cajun cooks firmly believe that adding warm or hot water will produce a pale roux.

    1/2 cup shortening (lard or butter)
    1/2 cup all-purpose flour

Heat the shortening in a heavy, black cast-iron skillet over medium heat. Add flour, stirring constantly. Cook until the roux begins to turn a light brown. Lower the heat and continue cooking and stirring until the roux is the desired degree of doneness. Sometimes it takes thirty minutes to an hour to make a good roux.

If a recipe calls for a light brown roux, this means the color of peanut butter. A dark brown roux will be the color of chocolate.

Cooked roux can be kept indefinitely in a covered jar. If the shortening separates, stir it back into the roux before you use it.

Cajun Ripe Olive Jambalaya

The Lord called thy name a green olive tree, fair and of goodly fruit.
    —Jeremiah 11:16

2 1/2 tablespoons virgin olive oil
1 clove garlic, mashed
1/2 cup onions, chopped
2 tablespoons bell pepper, chopped
3 ripe tomatoes, peeled and chopped
2 cups chicken broth
3/4 cup long-grain rice
1/2 bay leaf
1/8 teaspoon cloves
1/8 teaspoon fresh thyme
1 teaspoon salt
Dash cayenne pepper
1 1/2 cups fresh shrimp, cleaned
1/2 cup cooked, diced ham
1 cup ripe olives, coarsely chopped

In a deep saucepan heat the olive oil and sauté the fresh garlic, onions, and bell pepper. Cook until the onions are transparent. Add the tomatoes, chicken broth, rice, bay leaf, cloves, thyme, salt, and cayenne. Simmer for twenty minutes under a tight cover. Add the shrimp, ham, and olives. Cover and cook for ten minutes or until the rice is tender and the liquid is absorbed.

Little Bit's Brown Beef Stew with Potato Dumplings

1 1/2 pounds beef stew meat
2 tablespoons all-purpose flour
1/2 teaspoon salt
2 onions, sliced
2 tablespoons bacon drippings
3/4 cup water
1 tablespoon vinegar

3 medium-sized carrots, sliced
Potato dumplings
Handful of snipped fresh parsley

Combine the flour, salt, and pepper. Coat the meat with this mixture. In a heavy iron pot cook the beef and onions in bacon drippings until the onions are a golden brown and the meat is browned also. Stir in the water and vinegar and add the carrots. Bring to a boil, cover, and simmer for two hours or until the meat is tender. Drop the potato dumplings into the bubbling stew. Cover and simmer for an additional fifteen minutes. Sprinkle with fresh parsley before serving.

Potato Dumplings

Combine one beaten egg, three-fourths cup of soft bread crumbs, one tablespoon of all-purpose flour, one tablespoon of finely chopped onions, one tablespoon of snipped parsley, one-half teaspoon of salt, and a dash of pepper. Stir in two-and-a-half cups of finely shredded raw potato. With floured fingers, form small balls. Dust the balls with flour and drop them into the bubbling stew, according to directions.

Little Bit's Favorite Black Bean Soup

2 cups black beans
1/4 cup onions, chopped
4 tablespoons fresh butter
2 ribs celery, chopped
10 cups water
2 1/2 teaspoons salt
1 lemon, sliced paper thin
Dash black pepper
1/4 cup dry sherry
2 hard-boiled eggs, chopped

Soak the black beans overnight in enough water to cover them. Drain and rinse thoroughly. In a large iron kettle, cook the onions in the butter until they are tender but not brown. Add the beans, celery, and water.

Cook the beans for about three-and-a-half hours, slowly. Rub the beans with liquid through a strainer, getting them as smooth as possible. Stir in the salt and pepper. Heat the soup just to boiling and stir in the sherry just before serving. Top each bowl of soup with a chopped egg and a slice of lemon.

Little Bit's Bacon Popovers

4 slices bacon
1 cup milk
2 fresh eggs
1/2 teaspoon salt
1 cup sifted all-purpose flour
1/2 cup softened butter
1/8 teaspoon fresh oregano
1/8 teaspoon fresh sage

Preheat the oven to 475 degrees. Cook the bacon until it is crisp, drain, and reserve about one tablespoon of the drippings. Crumble the bacon and set it aside.

In a bowl combine the eggs and milk, then add the flour and salt. Beat until smooth. Add reserved bacon drippings and stir in the bacon.

Fill well-greased custard cups half full. Bake for fifteen minutes. Do not remove the popovers from the oven but reduce the heat to 350 degrees and continue baking for twenty-five to thirty minutes more, until the popovers are brown and firm.

Pierce the popovers with the tines of a fork before you remove them from the oven. Butter them with the fresh herb butter made from the three remaining ingredients.

Little Bit's Gumbo Filé

1 6-pound chicken
Salt and black pepper
1 large center-cut ham slice
1 tablespoon pure lard
Chicken fat

3 tablespoons flour
1/2 onion, finely chopped
1/2 tomato, cut into small pieces
1 1/2 quarts boiling water
1 bay leaf
3 sprigs fresh thyme
Dash cayenne pepper
2 dozen fresh oysters with juice
3 sprigs fresh parsley
3 tablespoons pure butter
1 tablespoon file powder

Clean and cut the chicken into small pieces. Sprinkle it with salt and pepper. Cut the ham into small pieces. Put the lard and some of the chicken fat into a saucepan, add the ham, and fry for about five minutes. Remove the ham from the fat, then fry the chicken, browning it on both sides but not cooking it thoroughly.

Take the browned chicken from the pan and add flour to the hot fat. Make a roux by stirring constantly to keep the mix from burning. Once the roux is brown, add the onions and brown them to a golden color. Add the tomato and let it cook for a few minutes. Add the boiling water gradually, then the ham, chicken, bay leaf, thyme, pepper, salt, and cayenne to taste. Set on a slow fire and cook until the meat is almost tender.

Then add the oysters, which have been washed in cold water to remove all particles of shell, the oyster juice, which should be strained, the chopped parsley, and the butter. Continue cooking for about fifteen minutes longer. Add the filé powder slowly, stirring well.

Serve over cooked rice.

Little Bit's Slow Scrambled Eggs

4 tablespoons salted butter
1/4 cup heavy cream
Dash salt (to taste)
Dash freshly ground white pepper
Fresh chives

Melt the butter in the top of a double boiler over low heat. Remove from the heat and let the butter cool for a few minutes. Return the double boiler to the heat and break the number of eggs you need to cook into the pot. Add the heavy cream. Cook slowly over simmering water, slowly folding the eggs into large curds. Remove from the heat, season with salt and white pepper, and a garnish with freshly cut chives. The chives give the egg a real tang.

Old-Fashioned Soda Bread

3 1/2 cups all-purpose flour
1/2 cup sugar
1/2 teaspoon baking soda
1 teaspoon salt
2 teaspoons baking powder
2 large eggs, beaten
1 pint sour cream
1 cup raisins

Preheat the oven to 350 degrees. Mix together the flour, sugar, salt, baking soda, and baking powder. Fold in the sour cream and the eggs. Add the raisins. Pour the batter into a well-greased eight-inch round cake pan. Bake for about one hour or until the loaf sounds hollow when tapped on the bottom. Cool on a wire rack. Serve with orange marmalade.

Apple Butter

2 pounds apples, Granny Smith or winesap
1 cup real apple cider
2 1/2 cups dark brown sugar
1 teaspoon ground cinnamon
1/4 teaspoon ground ginger
1/2 teaspoon cloves
1 teaspoon fresh lemon juice
1 tablespoon grated lemon rind
2 teaspoons port wine

Cut and core the apples, quarter, but do not peel. Mix them with the apple cider and cook until the apples are soft. Put the pulp through a fine strainer. For every cup of pulp, add one-half cup brown sugar. Add the remaining ingredients. Cook, stirring the mixture at a low simmer until the sugar is dissolved. Do not boil. Continue cooking until the apple butter starts to set. Place a small amount on a plate; when no liquid separates around the edge, it is done. Remove from heat and pour into sterilized glass canning jars. Pour hot paraffin over the top.

Little Bit's Sour Cream Pound Cake

1/2 cup butter, softened
1 cup sugar
3 whole eggs
1 3/4 cups flour
1 teaspoon baking soda
1 teaspoon ground cardamon
1 teaspoon ground cinnamon
1 cup sour cream
1 teaspoon pure vanilla extract

Preheat the oven to 350 degrees and grease a loaf pan well. Dust a little flour over the greased pan.

Cream the butter and sugar together until the mixture is light and fluffy. Beat in the eggs one at a time. Sift the flour with the baking soda, cinnamon, and cardamom, and stir half of the dry ingredients into the batter. Beat in the sour cream and the vanilla, then the rest of the dry ingredients.

Pour the contents into the pan and rap the pan sharply on the table to remove any air pockets. Bake in the center of the oven for about sixty minutes or until the top of the cake is golden brown and lightly spongy to the touch.

Corrie

Corrie Wolff was a light-colored quadroon who lived in a squatty cabin of whitewashed boards. The floor of the tiny porch was only one step up. The cabin sat behind the big house on "Tote Road," used during slavery days by servants returning to their quarters from the big house. "Toting" food and supplies from the master's kitchen was an accepted fact, never questioned by anyone. From that practice, the road took its name.

Corrie's father, Toby Wolff, had been a slave, and she also claimed to be a direct descendent of Dr. Yah Yah, a New Orleans voodoo doctor in the mid-nineteenth century. Most of her cooking did reflect a New Orleans background.

Corrie's hair was a neat black cap of rough velvet, covering the immaculate outline of her skull. She swore this style was inspired by an ancient tribal cropping. Imbedded in her life were a great many of the old customs. She always oiled her body, rubbing until it gleamed like a sheath of black steel. Her bosom was the most comforting refuge possible for a broken-hearted child.

Corrie's little cabin was the sort of place children begged to be allowed to go to eat and to sleep on the deep shuck-filled mattress and sweet down pillows, the kind of place where a child could poke a hole in the side of a cold biscuit and pour molasses in it or sit smothered in the big bed and eat a fill of fresh collard greens with the pot liquor and corn pone or let Corrie pull sweet potatoes, bleeding sugar sweet juices, from the persimmon-colored coals that would soon turn to warm ashes white as frost.

Sook would say to us, "You think I don't know you take that baby Truman and go traipsing down to Corrie's house at night?" Children brought up in the South were weaned on tales of ghosts, haints, spirits, and plat-eyes. Corrie was one of the most delightful sources for tales of witches, devils, and bad-luck omens, and we couldn't stay away.

She knew how to make a point, that's for sure. She would say, "Trees has spirits same as man. Dead trees are best left alone. God made them to stand up after they die." Or, "Ebb tide is a dangerous time for sick people. When the river's tide turns, life can go quickly." She would warn, "A wrong name will kill a baby."

Corrie saw a sign in everything. "Don't ever eat in a toilet, 'cause you is feedin' the devil an' starvin' God."

"If you wants rain, sweep down the cobwebs in the house, or you can build a fire in a stump on a cloudy day."

"Give me the signs every time," she would say, "'cause black people rule sickness with magic, while white folks gets sick and die. White folks leave money to their children; black people leaves signs. Give me the signs every time."

Our great love and respect for animals came from Corrie and Sook. We were taught that there was something companionable about animals. Corrie always had an assortment of odd pets. She told us of the time she heard this terrible ruckus out in her chicken yard and found a strange sight. The chicken fence had been knocked down, and an ornery, low-down, red razorback hog was in the pen. He was dirty, lean, and mean. His red hair was stiff, covered with muck and caked with mud. He was a sneaky, no-mannered beast. Corrie took to him right away. She told us, "Why, child, that hog was so pore a body could hang a hat on his hips."

Corrie named him "Red Rip" and soon found a use for him. She tied a rope around his neck and took him squealing and pulling with her to hunt blackberries. His squealing scared the snakes away.

The animals of Corrie's we liked best were twin coons. She found them under a palmetto tree, huddled up and cold after a heavy rainstorm. The mother had obviously been carried away by the waters, so Corrie carried the baby coons home. They were identical, with their little iron-gray bodies and strange inquisitive black-masked faces, except one seemed to have a face that was more serene than the other.

Remembering the old saying, "When animals are twins, one will have a mean eye and the other will have a kind eye," Corrie named them accordingly: Roscoe for the mean eye and Sweet William for the kind one. She certainly didn't go wrong. In *Other Voices, Other Rooms*, Truman used Corrie's idea about twins when he wrote about Florabel and Idabel: "We were born twins, like I told you, but Mama says the Lord always sends something bad with the good."

The old story that coons are the cleanest animals in the world is untrue. Roscoe never washed anything. He loved dirt. He was too greedy to take the time to wash food. Sweet William tried to wash his, but he had to hurry or Roscoe would take it away from him. Often, Sweet William had to rely on human help to fend off his greedy twin.

At first, they were fed out of a bottle, rich jersey milk from Corrie's cow. Within a few days they had learned to lie on their backs and balance the bottle on their stomachs with their hind paws, gripping the top with their forepaws. When Roscoe finished his warm milk, he would chew the nipple to shreds. Sweet William would let his empty bottle gently slide from his mouth, roll over, and sleep. When Roscoe was punished for chewing the nipples, he bit the living stew out of the punisher's hand. When Sweet William was scolded, he would cry pitifully like a child.

Usually it is a simple matter to house-train a coon, but not in Roscoe's case. No. He refused to be housebroken. He knew what he was doing, and he did it on purpose. He hated women and waited for them to come calling on Sunday in their best clothes. He would amiably climb onto their shoulders and trick them into believing he was cute and cunning. Then . . . he *knew* what he was doing!

Sweet William liked to curl around the neck of a person in genuine affection. He never played tricks. The only affection Roscoe ever showed was to sit in your lap and nibble at your ear, but if he was denied his way, his little teeth would suddenly turn into hypodermic needles.

A coon will eat almost anything a human eats. Roscoe's favorite dish was soft scrambled eggs, but if they weren't just right, he would growl menacingly and stomp his feet in a furious sort of way. Corrie would hurry to replace the offending dish with something more to his liking.

Corrie was old, and every night before retiring she would make herself a "bub," as she called it. This was an old custom among Southern gentlewomen. A bub is made with heavy cream and whiskey or wine and served in a silver or very thin glass goblet. Corrie had many years before removed one of the silver goblets from the dining room in the house and carried it back to her home on the Tote Road. The goblet was for her personal use, and no one ever questioned its removal.

The first time she had a bub after acquiring Roscoe and Sweet William, she brought the drink out and sat in her favorite chair while Truman and several other children were piled on top of her bed, enjoying hot fried cakes and cherry Cokes. Roscoe jumped up in her lap and reached with his little almost human hands to see what was in the shiny goblet. Most animals turn their heads in disgust at the smell of alcohol. Not Roscoe.

He growled when Corrie tried to stop him, so she put the bub up to his pointed nose. He clutched the stem of the goblet and in one long gulp drank its contents. Then he licked the goblet's sides. It was all over in only a moment.

Shortly, he jumped down from Corrie's lap, his eyes crossed and his little legs folded up, unable to support him. He wobbled all around, cross-eyed as an owl, then staggered off. Corrie found him sleeping it off in the middle of the kitchen table, where he had drunk some milk left there and apparently bathed in it, too, because there were milk tracks all over the kitchen floor.

Corrie told us that early the next morning, before she had gone into the kitchen, she heard a pattering of little feet. Roscoe came swaggering out. His shoulders were hunched like a prizefighter's, daring anyone to correct him. His whole bearing was that of a bully. He was cold sober and pleased with himself.

The relationship between a coon and other family pets is remarkable. The dog, Splash, was a serious, rabbit-colored dog with a split ear and a drooping eye and a foolish stump of a tail. Corrie said he was a "no-account, lazy dog" that spent his time playing so strenuously with Roscoe that the poor creature would come whimpering and praying with his eyes to Corrie to spare him, beating the floor plut-plut-plut with his stump of a tail to protect himself from further damage at the hands of the indefatigable small ball of fur who gnawed unmercifully on his legs and tail.

Corrie's cat, Ginger, was a huge, battle-scarred tomcat that, due to a diagonal scar, seemed always to be grinning. He was flat-eared, with a long tail and a nasty disposition. He and Roscoe had little in common, and Ginger was too smart for Roscoe, so they remained the most distant of friends.

When Truman left Monroeville to go to New York to join his mother, Corrie told him, "You know, child, I loves you till the end of the numbers." Her strong love and her good cooking were integral to the Faulk way of life."

Corrie's Creole Chicory Coffee

8 sugar cubes
5 whole cloves
2 cinnamon sticks, broken in small pieces
2 tablespoons minced orange peel
1 1/2 teaspoons coriander seed (optional)
2 teaspoons minced lemon peel
1 bay leaf
1 cup brandy
1/4 cup curacao
4 cups fresh brewed dark-roast New Orleans-style coffee with chicory

Heat the sugar, cloves, cinnamon, lemon and orange peels, bay leaf, and coriander in a shallow pan over medium heat. Mash together the ingredients with the back of a spoon.

Pour the brandy and curacao into a corner of the pan, heat briefly, and ignite. When the flame is high, stir in the coffee. Cover to extinguish the flame. Throw away the bay leaf. Serve immediately.

"Barefoot coffee" is coffee without cream and sugar.

Corrie's Louisiana Bayou Chili

1/2 pound very spicy sausage
3 pounds coarsely ground lean beef
15 ounces tomato juice (fresh or canned)
1 large onion, chopped fine
1 clove fresh garlic, chopped fine
Several dashes Tabasco
1 tablespoon salt
1 tablespoon paprika
1 tablespoon cumin seed
3 heaping tablespoons chili powder
1 teaspoon freshly ground black pepper
1 cup red wine
1/2 cup water
2 1/2 tablespoons flour

Chop the sausage into small bits. Cook the sausage and ground beef together, stirring constantly, in a heavy iron pot until the meat turns gray. Skim off all excess fat.

Add all the other ingredients except the flour. Use enough red wine, mixed with an equal amount of water, to cover the mixture. Allow this to simmer, stirring regularly for about one-and-a-half hours.

Make a paste of flour and a small amount of water and add this to the pot. Continue stirring for another fifteen minutes. Serve over cooked rice.

Curds and Cream

This is a famous Louisiana everyday meal. Set sour or raw milk in a crock until it becomes clabber. Pour it slowly into a curd press (a colander lined with a double thickness of cheesecloth may be used) until the press is full. Place the press in a pan and let it drain overnight. Turn into a flat dish, grate nutmeg freely over the top, and serve with fresh heavy sweet cream, more grated nutmeg, and sugar sprinklings.

Oysters Louisianne

1 dozen fresh oysters
3 tablespoons butter
2 tablespoons red pepper, chopped
2 tablespoons onion, chopped
3 tablespoons flour
Few grains cayenne
Salt and pepper to taste

Parboil the oysters, remove them from the pan, reserve the liquid, and add enough water to make one-and-a-half cups. Melt the butter and fry the onion and red pepper together. Gradually pour this mixture on the liquid and stir constantly. Bring to the boiling point and season. Arrange the oysters on a platter, pour the liquid over them, and bake for fifteen minutes in an oven set at 325 degrees until the oysters and heated and their edges have curled.

Omelet of the Bayou

1 cup fresh crabmeat
1 stalk fresh celery, chopped fine
1/2 teaspoon salt
1/2 green bell pepper, chopped fine
1 small onion
1/2 teaspoon freshly ground black pepper
1/2 teaspoon paprika
3 eggs, separated
Oil for cooking

Mix the crabmeat, salt, celery, green peppers, and onions with the egg yolks. Beat the egg whites until they are very stiff and pour them over the other ingredients. Mix lightly after adding black pepper and paprika. Cook in a small amount of oil in a heavy iron skillet until brown. Turn and cook the other side. The best method is to fold the omelet in half.

Creole Herb Omelet

3 very small green onions, chopped fine
1 1/4 tablespoons fresh parsley, chopped
6 fresh mushrooms, finely chopped
1 dozen fresh eggs
6 ounces fresh butter
1/2 teaspoon fresh oregano
1/2 teaspoon fresh sweet marjoram

Sauté the mushrooms, onions, and parsley in two ounces of butter. Cook until tender. Break the eggs into a bowl and add the oregano and marjoram. Beat well. Melt the balance of the butter in a large frying pan. Add the eggs and the onion mixture. Cook until soft. Roll and serve. This makes an omelet large enough for five or six people.

Corrie's New Orleans Pralines

These pralines are called white pralines because they aren't made in the customary way, using brown sugar.

2 cups sugar
1 teaspoon soda
1 cup buttermilk
2 tablespoons pure butter
2 1/2 cups brown pecan pieces
1 teaspoon pure vanilla extract
About 26 pecan halves

Combine the sugar, soda, buttermilk, and butter in a heavy iron pot. Cook over a high heat for five minutes, stirring constantly. Add the broken pecan pieces, and cook, stirring constantly, over medium heat until the mixture reaches 230 degrees. Remove from the heat and add vanilla. Beat until the mixture begins to thicken.

Drop the mixture by the spoonful on a buttered marble slab or waxed paper. Place a whole pecan on top of each praline. Store in an airtight container to allow the pralines to mellow. This receipt makes about two dozen pralines.

Corrie's Bread Pudding

I sent this receipt to Joanne Carson after Truman's death, at her request.

2 cups whole milk
1/2 stick butter
1/2 cup sugar
4 cups cubed, day-old bread
1/2 cup raisins
2 eggs, well beaten
1/8 teaspoon salt
1/2 teaspoon freshly ground nutmeg
1 teaspoon pure vanilla extract
Brandy Sauce

Preheat the oven to 350 degrees. Melt the butter in the milk, which has been scalded. Pour the mixture over the bread and raisins. Let this stand about fifteen minutes. Add the eggs, nutmeg, salt, and vanilla. Bake in a well-greased pan or dish for thirty-five to forty minutes. Serve the pudding with hot Brandy Sauce.

BRANDY SAUCE
1 stick butter
2 cups powdered sugar
1/4 cup aged brandy

Cream the butter and sugar together and gradually add the brandy.

Corrie's Cajun Ginger Cake

1 cup oil
1 cup sugar
3 tablespoons black molasses
1 cup sugar-cane syrup
2 1/8 cups flour
1/2 teaspoon baking powder
3 eggs
1 teaspoon baking soda

3/4 cup hot water
1 teaspoon cinnamon
1 teaspoon ginger

Preheat the oven to 350 degrees. Beat together sugar, oil, sugar-cane syrup, and molasses. Combine this mixture with the flour and baking powder. Add the eggs one at a time, stirring well after each addition. Mix the baking soda and hot water; add, along with the ginger and cinnamon, to the batter and mix well. Pour in a greased baking pan and bake about forty minutes.

Corrie's Fresh Blackberry Cobbler

Blackberrying in July was a daily routine rather than a recreational pastime. All you had to do was follow the meandering paths of ripening berries across cornfields, fences, and creeks, never tarrying too long in one spot, lest the big juicy ones in another patch be missed.

1 pint fresh blackberries
1 cup flour
2 teaspoons baking powder
1 cup sugar
2 eggs
3/4 cup milk
1 teaspoon pure vanilla
1 teaspoon grated lemon rind
1 1/2 cups heavy cream, chilled
2 tablespoons pounded, crushed sugar

Preheat the oven to 350 degrees. Wash the blackberries in a pierced-bottom bowl under cold running water. Discard any stems and blemished berries. Spread the berries on a linen towel and pat them completely dry. Pour the berries into a fresh bowl and set them aside.

Sift the flour and baking powder into a large mixing bowl and add the sugar, eggs, milk, vanilla, and lemon rind. With a wooden spoon, beat the ingredients until they are completely mixed. Pour the batter over the berries and bake in the center of the oven for one hour or until the top is brown. Remove the cobbler from the oven and let it sit while the cream is whipped.

With a whisk, beat the cream until it foams. Beat in the pounded sugar and continue to beat until the cream forms soft peaks. Serve the cobbler with the whipped cream.

Real Southern Cornbread

Mark Twain once said, "The North thinks it knows how to make cornbread, but this is a mere superstition." An old slave saying celebrated the importance of cornbread as a just reward for a hard day's work: "Carry dat load on your head/De Lord will bless your good cornbread." Cornbread and clabber was a favorite breakfast dish among the Creoles in New Orleans.

> 1 teaspoon sugar
> 2 cups fresh buttermilk
> 1 teaspoon baking powder
> 2 eggs
> 2 cups white cornmeal
> 1 teaspoon salt

Preheat the oven to 450 degrees. Heat a greased pan in the oven until it is sizzling hot. Beat the eggs with the buttermilk. In a separate bowl, stir the soda, cornmeal, and salt. Add the egg mixture to the dry ingredients. Bake twenty to twenty-five minutes.

Corrie's Collard Greens with Cornmeal Cakes

> 1 large bunch fresh collards
> 2 teaspoons salt
> 1 teaspoon sugar
> 3 slices bacon
> 1 small ham hock
> 1 cup cornmeal
> 1 pod red pepper
> Hot liquid from collards

Wash and trim the collards. Place them in a big pan and cover them well with water. Add the salt, sugar, and bacon, along with the drippings and the ham hock. Cover and bring to a boil. Add the red pepper. Simmer until the collards are tender.

Combine the cornmeal (with additional salt if desired). Add enough hot broth to make a stiff batter. Shape the batter into thick little cakes (about one-half inch thick). Be sure the collards are still well covered with water. Lay the corn cakes on top of the collards; boil gently until the cakes are cooked inside.

Serve the corn cakes on top of the collards, along with pieces of ham and bacon. Pour the pot liquor on top of the corn cakes.

Corrie's Creole Salad

4 cups cooked macaroni (about 1/2 pound raw)
2 cups diced tomatoes
1 cup sharp cheese, grated
1 cup mayonnaise
1/4 cup sliced stuffed olives
2 tablespoons grated onion
1/2 clove garlic, finely chopped
1/8 teaspoon cayenne pepper

Boil the macaroni in salt water until tender but not mushy, rinse well in cold water, drain, cut into one-inch pieces, and place on cheesecloth to drain and chill. Make sure that it is very cold. Mix the chilled macaroni with the other ingredients and serve on lettuce.

Corrie's New Orleans Rice Cakes

These are the crustiest and most delicious fried cakes in the whole world. In New Orleans they were called calas and sold on the streets by vendors who chanted the following poem:

> We sell it to the rich, we sell it to the poor,
> We give it to the sweet brownskin peepin' out the door.
> Tout chaud, Madame, tout chaud!
> Git 'em while they're hot! Hot calas!

One cup of coffee, fifteen cents calas,
Make you smile the live-long day.
Calas, tout chauds, Madame, tout chauds!
Git 'em while they're hot! Hot calas!

1 1/2 cups hot cooked rice
1 cake fresh yeast
1/2 cup warm water
3 eggs, beaten
1 1/4 cups all-purpose flour
1/4 cup sugar
1/2 teaspoon salt
1/4 teaspoon fresh ground nutmeg
Butter or oil
Sifted powdered sugar

Mash the rice grains and allow them to cool to lukewarm. Dissolve the yeast (one package of dry yeast can be substituted) in the warm water and add it to the rice. Cover and let rise overnight in a warm place.

Add the eggs, sugar, salt, and nutmeg to the rice mixture, beating until smooth. Cover and let stand again in a warm place for about thirty minutes. Put about three inches of either butter or oil in a heavy iron pot. Let it get almost smoking hot. Drop rice dough with a tablespoon into the fat and cook to a golden brown. This takes about three minutes. Drain and sprinkle with powdered sugar. Eat at once.

Corrie's Famous Herb Chicken

Get a really plump fowl and cut it into quarters. Dry the pieces off with a linen towel and sprinkle them lightly with flour. Brown the pieces in butter over a hot flame, being careful not to burn the butter. As the chicken is browning, sprinkle it lightly with a pinch each of rosemary, tarragon, sage, and thyme as finely crushed as possible. Turn the flame down low and continue cooking until the chicken is tender.

Place the cooked chicken on a platter, skim off the fat from the cooking pan, and add three-quarters of a cup of fine white wine. Simmer the wine until the sauce thickens. Then pour it over the chicken. Sprinkle fresh parsley lightly over the top and serve immediately.

Chicken and Dumplings

This recipe, according to Corrie, came from a slave who cooked on a plantation in Tazewell, Virginia.

    1 large stewing chicken (about 6 pounds)
    1 1/2 quarts cold water
    Salt and pepper to taste

Put the chicken in a large stockpot and cover with cold water. Season to taste. Cover the pot, bring to a boil, and simmer until done. Pour off three or four cups of broth to make the gravy.

DUMPLINGS

    1 cup regular flour
    1 1/2 teaspoons baking powder
    1/2 teaspoon salt
    2 tablespoons butter or pure lard
    1/2 cup sweet milk

Mix the dry ingredients with the shortening. Stir in the milk. On a floured board, roll the dough out to a thickness of about one-eighth of an inch. Cut the dough into strips about an inch wide. Cover and steam the dumplings for about fifteen minutes, then remove and drape over the sliced chicken.

GRAVY

    3 cups of chicken broth (fat not skimmed off)
    1 tablespoon butter
    3 tablespoons flour
    Salt and pepper to taste

Heat the broth in a frying skillet. Add the butter. Mix the flour with enough water to make a thin paste. Stir the flour mixture into the broth and season to taste with salt and pepper. Cook the gravy until it is as thick as heavy cream. Pour it over the chicken and dumplings.

Sem Muscadine

Sem was a cook of extraordinary talents and was always called upon for special occasions. He always came dressed in his "misbehavin' coat," a frock tailcoat he had inherited from one of the plantation gentlemen. When he walked, it stood straight out in the wind and slapped him from behind.

Bringing Sem to town was quite a journey. Usually a car picked him up and returned him home after he had cooked his masterpieces. He lived across the river on an old plantation that had long been unoccupied. Its innumerable windows appeared blank and bleak; its exterior, cold and forbidding. Sem lived "sort of" in the middle of one of the rooms that still had a roof. He refused to leave because as a boy he had lived on the plantation and had seen all the children desert the old place. The only labor he did around the place was to keep the private cemetery in the backyard weeded and planted with flowers each spring.

Some people thought Sem odd, and children made believe that they were scared of him. However, they never missed an opportunity to go and see him either. The old plantation still had twenty or thirty peafowls, with their beautiful greenish iridescent plumage and colors of a thousand eyes. They paraded on top of the rail fence or admired themselves in a pool of water.

To see Sem's white mice was always a treat for young visitors. He had bought them in Mobile, and they were as white as snow, with pink eyes and pink feet. Even the insides of their pointed little ears had a pale pinkness about them. All children, especially Truman, loved these gentle, sleek creatures.

When Sem came to do special affairs, he always brought a gift of something, mainly a tin bucket filled with swamp honey and a gallon of home-brew for Little Bit. He had high hopes of marrying Little Bit.

Sem was not a big man. He walked with a turkey-gobbler strut as he twirled his gold-headed cane that had been a gift to him many years earlier. His nose was flat and wide as a buckwheat cake, and his face was so wrinkled that it gave the impression that he saw the world through crumpled cobwebs. On his head he wore a high beaver hat so pale that it was almost white. You would never see Sem without his beaver, winter or summer.

When he arrived, Sem headed for Little Bit's kitchen, and we all followed. It was always a gay, happy time when Sem came because we knew it meant a big party or a "to do." We liked weddings and funerals least and fish-fry suppers on the banks of the Little River best of all.

Truman was probably the most inquisitive, being the youngest, and even then his imagination ran wild. He demanded of Sem, without waiting for an answer: "How are the mice? How is your pet buzzard, Icabard? Can I go home with you to pick fresh dewberries?"

Little Bit could stand it just so long and finally she would say, "Chile, you talks too much. Ifen God had wanted for you to talk so much he'd give you two moufs an' one ear, 'stead of two ears an' one mouf."

This pleased Sem because he wanted the kids to leave so he could be alone with Little Bit. He would start twirling his gold cane around and break into a song:

> A boy is like a dip of snuff,
> Take one sip, and that's enough.

Sem's actions didn't go over very well with Little Bit. It was perfectly right for her to correct Truman but not for Sem to do so.

She looked Sem straight in the eyes and said, "Don't never let yore faultin' fall on my ears or I will whop you up side of yore head so hard it will bust like a maypop."

After a few minutes, as her anger mounted, she slammed the kitchen door on her way out and said over her shoulder, "You're trash, an' you's triflin,' an' you's ugly! Stay out of my kitchen." Then discharging a final withering message, "An' furthermore you stinks!"

Sem smiled and said to the children, "Little Bit is just like one of dem big pussycats. Lots of times when you think she is fightin,' she lovin.'"

Truman writes about Sem in *Other Voices, Other Rooms:* "Down by the mailbox he ran into Zoo, and she was not alone, but stood talking with a short bullet-headed negro. It was Little Sunshine, the hermit . . . and [he was] ugly. He had a blue cataract in one eye, hardly a tooth in his head, and smelled bad; while she was in the kitchen Amy kept the gloved hand over her nose like a sachet handkerchief."

Sem's recipe for coffee was a poem:

> Black as sin,
> Hot as hell,
>
> Pure as an Angel,
> Sweet as love.

Sem's Oyster Stuffing

3/4 cup butter
2 tablespoons onion, chopped
3 tablespoons fresh parsley, chopped
1 1/2 cups fresh celery, chopped
6 cups soft breadcrumbs
1 pint fresh oysters
Salt and pepper to taste

Melt the butter and in it cook the onions, parsley, and celery. Add the breadcrumbs and heat well. Add the chopped oysters and season. This is delicious stuffing for birds or turkeys.

Little River Fried Catfish

Sem claimed that our catfish had slept in the Little River the night before we ate them.

6 average-sized fresh catfish
1/4 teaspoon fresh black pepper
1 teaspoon salt
2 cups yellow water-ground cornmeal
Pure lard for frying

Sprinkle the catfish with salt and pepper. Put the cornmeal in a brown paper bag. Drop in one fish at a time and be sure it gets well coated. Fry in deep lard (375 degrees) until golden brown. Drain and serve piping hot.

Sem's Tiny Lemon Tarts

These tarts were made especially for weddings and afternoon teas.

3/4 cup sugar
1 1/2 tablespoons cornstarch
1 1/2 tablespoons plain flour
Dash salt
3/4 cup water
2 eggs, slightly beaten
1 tablespoon butter
1/2 tablespoon fresh lemon rind, grated
1/2 cup fresh lemon juice
12 2-inch pastry shells, baked
Whipped cream

Combine the sugar, cornstarch, flour, and salt in a saucepan. Gradually add the water, stirring well. Cook over a low heat, stirring constantly, until the mixture is thick and bubbly. Gradually stir about one-quarter of the hot mixture into the eggs. Add this mix to the remaining hot mixture, stirring constantly. Cook for three minutes over a low heat, continuing to stir.

Remove the mixture from the heat and add the butter, lemon rind, and lemon juice. Stir until the butter melts. Cool slightly and spoon into the pastry shells. Garnish each tart with a dollop of whipped cream.

CRUST FOR TARTS

1 fresh egg yolk
1 1/2 tablespoons whipping cream
1/4 teaspoon almond extract
1/4 teaspoon salt
4 ounces unsalted butter
1 tablespoon ice water

1/2 teaspoon vanilla extract

1 1/2 cups all-purpose flour

1 1/2 tablespoons granulated sugar

This is a tender and crisp crust, and it is best to make the pastry ahead and refrigerate it for at least twenty-four hours before using it. The pastry must be rolled paper-thin with a light touch.

Cut the cold, firm butter into about ten pieces. Combine the egg yolk, ice water, whipping cream, and vanilla and almond extracts in a small bowl. Refrigerate.

Place the dry ingredients in a large mixing bowl, add the butter, and with a fork or pastry blender, cut the butter in until the mixture resembles coarse crumbs. Then stir the cold egg mixture in with a fork.

Now turn the dough out onto a work surface and press it together to form a ball. Wrap the ball in waxed paper and refrigerate it for about two hours. When you are ready to shape the crust, have your small tart-shell pans ready. Roll the dough as thin as possible, cut it into circles, being sure to leave about one-half inch for an overhang for each shell.

Fold one-quarter of the overhang toward the center of the shell to make a narrow hem extending about one-quarter inch above the rim of the pan. Press gently to make the shell smooth. Pierce holes in the bottom of the shell with fork. Refrigerate the shells in the pans for at least thirty minutes before baking.

Preheat the oven to 400 degrees. Before you start baking the shells, it is a good idea to line them with a small piece of aluminum foil, shiny side up. Fill the foil with dried beans and bake for about twenty minutes. Remove the foil and the beans and continue baking for an additional five minutes, until the bottom of the shell begins to color lightly.

Satan's Figs Flambé

When Sem prepared this dish, the whole family and the guests gathered and looked on in fascination at his showmanship.

25 fresh figs

4 tablespoons sugar

1 cup heated curacao

3/4 cup heated brandy

Peel the fresh figs and prick each several times with the tines of a silver fork. Place the figs in a large silver serving dish and sprinkle them with the sugar. Pour the curacao and brandy over the figs and light with a match. Shake the pan until the flame dies out.

Charity and Sylvester

Sharecroppers on six hundred acres of Bud Faulk's land, Charity and Sylvester hosted an annual Fourth of July picnic that produced many of the happiest moments of our childhoods.

The path to their house ran close to enormous live oaks standing at regular intervals, all of them festooned with trailing moss that made a weird roof overhead during the walk. The house was a three-room log cabin facing the cotton fields, its back door going down to the bank of the Little River. The windows were shuttered. The roof was made of cypress shingles that had begun to curl at the ends from age. A chimney on one side of the house poured out thick black smoke, winter or summer.

The yard was always swept clean, with only the prints from the chickens' feet marring its perfection. All the trees were whitewashed about halfway up their trunks. Confederate and yellow jasmines sprawled over the top of the little cabin, casting tendrils every which way and knitting the air into a green curtain.

When the fabulous Fourth finally arrived, the morning heat would always make the leaves on the trees leading to the cabin limp, but that couldn't dampen our spirits on this perfect day. The picnic was strictly a family affair, held on the banks of the river.

The only outsider invited was Reverend Woot. He was fat and easy to laugh. He was so educated he could read Scripture right out of the book. He always consumed every variety of food and drink set before him (especially hot biscuits) with unabashed gusto. He had a master-piece of a nose that any artist would have given his life to paint. We all enjoyed his tales, up to a point. When he started off "But you know what . . . " and would tell about people splitting in half, blood running from the eyes, or people screaming themselves mute because of their sins, we had had enough. He consumed fried chicken so fast that his moustache looked like his eyebrows had slipped.

As we rode up to the cabin, Sylvester came to the door. He was not a happy man. He moved brooding in a cloud of dark meditation. He was tall and coal black, with rounded shoulders and a head that dropped forward. His hair was kinky and cut short, leaving him a goodly stretch of shining forehead. He and Grandpa Bud had been friends since Bud found him living on a river bank in 1886 and brought him to live on Faulk land.

Charity's mother had been part Indian. Charity had an eager hooded gaze that was referred to as "the Indian look." She was a big woman and had the Indian manner of royalty. She was a tall, still handsome octoroon with pale yellow skin and the noble bearing of a woman who, in youth, had carried baskets on an upright head. Her large, heavy, composed face, in which disposition had long since triumphed over contour and feature, appeared to hang there like a moon in a sullen sky. Her spreading figure, unconfined by an old-fashioned calico dress, seemed to fill the entire space of the chair. Her behind looked like a cushion with the stuffing coming out.

When he was young, Truman always classified women by their breasts. There were the cabbages, the rosebuds, and the hound-dog ears. Charity was in the latter group.

The most charming thing about Charity was the way her smile seemed to begin first in her eyes, so deep and changeable in color, then ripple on and linger in an edge of light on her lips.

Charity was hard to explain. Sometimes she was kind and tender; others, hard and unrelenting. The minute Truman would put his foot on her steps, she would admonish him to "wash your hands 'cause they are dirty as possum paws." She had a sort of sultriness that whipped around in the air like a thunderstorm ready to break. We all attributed this to the Indian in her. Sometimes she acted as if her nerves had been drawn through a keyhole, but on the Fourth of July she was happy and gracious to a fault.

An empty hogshead, got from the store in town, was half filled with water from the spring at the picnic ground. Fresh lemons were cut and squeezed and added. A great muslin bag full of sugar was poured in. Then a huge block of ice was stripped out of its croker sack, washed clean of sawdust, and dumped into the hogshead with the lemons and sugar and water. A bucket filled with ice was studded with fresh mint for tea and for the lemonade. Sylvester used a long, clean hickory paddle to mix the lemonade. He leaned over the hogshead and stirred vigorously, and the lemonade was ready for the picnic.

Of course, today I believe in a safe and sane Fourth of July and am grateful that children do not lose fingers from five-inch salutes or eyes to misfiring Roman candles. But in my heart I mourn that wonderful, insane, sometimes violent day of celebration from my childhood. Handling firecrackers, setting off rockets, blasting tin cans into the air, somehow we were close to that dangerous original event that gave us the cause of celebration. It seemed right to take that risk.

The greatest thrill of all, perhaps, was the early morning visit to the blacksmith shop, before the picnic. There the blacksmith, Buzz Carrabee, powerful and proud of his brawny arms and his split leather apron, already blackened around the face, would put a big charge of powder on an anvil. Then he would insert a fuse and put another anvil on top of that. When the fuse was ignited, the powder blew up with a tremendous roar and a crash of iron, blasting indignant citizens from their beds, sending dogs howling under porches and bushes, terrifying horses so that they stamped their shod fee and whinnied from the barn.

After the adventure with the anvils, we scattered to burn up in a short time the fireworks we had bought with our painfully acquired money, earned by selling junk and lemonade and by mowing lawns. All over town the squandering of our savings went on. There were the red "sons-o-guns," which sputtered and cracked when you rubbed them over the sidewalks. They would go tearing into a body's legs if you dropped a rock on them. And there would be the delicate splatter of tiny "ladyfingers" firing. We would hold whole strings of these, light them, then throw them in the air to catch in trees and carry on a private spitting war against each other.

After the firecracker blast, we went off to another two hours designed to test our courage and foolhardiness, that furious trial by food called the Fourth of July picnic. A collection of treasures made from Charity's best receipts was spread out on the banks of the river as if a regiment were momentarily expected. All of it would be from her own kitchen: fried chicken, pickles, watermelon, pans of biscuits with tubs of butter, fried catfish from the washpot every few minutes, gingerbread, fresh coconut ice cream, country ham, deviled eggs, fresh shrimp, potato salad, lemonade, iced tea, coffee, and Coca-Cola.

After eating, we all swooshed down the river on inner tubes. On an inner tube you don't just float. You bounce a little. You get out of the current momentarily, and you paddle madly to get back into it. You hit a small whirlpool, then go round and round like a phonograph record. Without a doubt, inner-tubing is the most rollicking sport since the rumble seat became extinct!

Finally, the day ended as any celebration of a time of danger and triumph should end. Exhausted, dirty, bandaged, and blistered, we struggled off to bed. The country was safe for another year, and so were we.

In the South, when you hear the whippoorwill,
it is time to go barefooted.

Sylvester's Smoked Country Ham

There is an old saying that a good country ham "ought to be spicy as a woman's tongue, sweet as her kiss, and tender as her love."

The pigs that Sylvester raised on the old Faulk plantation were carefully tended and fed only on peanuts, which gave them a delicious flavor. He always kept a ham in the smokehouse for the Fourth of July.

His hams were smoked over hickory wood in a closed smokehouse, then heavily salted and hung on hooks. They usually weighed around twelve pounds.

Wash a smoked ham with a stiff brush, using hot water. Put the ham in a boiler of water deep enough so that the ham floats. When the water boils, turn the flame to a very low heat. Don't let the water bubble. Cook until the meat turns loose from the bone. Take the ham out of the boiler. Do not leave it standing in the water. When the ham is cool, skin it and trim off some of the fat. Put the skinned, trimmed ham in a hot oven so that it will brown very quickly, in about ten minutes.

Fried Catfish

The main food at the Fourth of July picnic was fried fresh catfish. A big iron washpot with a roaring fire underneath, fed by fat lighter knots, was filled half full of pure lard, which was heated till it was *very* hot. The following receipt can be used for any amount of fish.

1 cup all-purpose flour
1 teaspoon salt
1/8 teaspoon freshly ground black pepper
2 eggs, slightly beaten

Heat the oil to about 375 degrees. Mix the flour, salt, and pepper and coat the fish with this mixture. Dip the coated fish into the eggs, then again into the flour (or into dry breadcrumbs if you want the fish crunchy). Catfish usually take about four minutes to cook a golden brown.

Southern fishermen know that it's good luck to spit tobacco juice on a fish hook before lowering it into the water. They also know that it is bad luck to step over a fishing pole or to step on a fishing line. It is deadly to let two poles cross.

Baking Powder Biscuits

1/2 cup butter
2 cups all-purpose flour
1 tablespoon sugar
3 teaspoons baking powder
1 teaspoon salt
1/8 teaspoon fresh sage
3/4 cup milk

Preheat the oven to 450 degrees. Cut the butter into the flour, sugar, baking powder, and salt. Mix until you have the texture of a coarse meal. Stir in the milk until the dough leaves the sides of the bowl.

The dough will be rather sticky and soft. Add the sage and blend that into the dough.

Turn the dough onto a lightly floured surface. Lightly knead the dough about six or seven times. Roll or pat the dough to a one-half-inch thickness. Cut with a biscuit cutter.

Place the biscuits on an ungreased cookie sheet about one inch apart for crusty sides; for soft sides, let the biscuits touch. Bake until golden brown, about ten or fifteen minutes. This will make about a dozen biscuits. Butter them while they are hot.

Charity's Fresh Coconut Ice Cream

George Washington is said to have possessed the first ice cream freezer in America. Thomas Jefferson also purchased one in 1784. He called it a "cream machine for ice." (Jefferson, known in his day as a great epicure, also introduced macaroni and vanilla into this country.)

With such impressive historical credentials, it is entirely appropriate that the ice cream freezer was such an integral part of our Fourth of July celebration. No such party is complete without its freezer full of homemade cream.

Charity always sent to Mobile to get her fresh coconuts for the picnic. She said the only way to get true coconut flavor was to use a fresh whole coconut. That must be true because she made the best ice cream that ever passed a person's lips.

1 average-sized coconut with milk
2 cups scalded milk
3 egg yolks
3/4 cup sugar
Pinch salt
2 cups heavy cream
2 tablespoons pure almond extract

With a hammer and a nail, tap holes in the three eyes of the coconut, drain out the liquid, and reserve. Split the coconut and pry out the meat. Grate the meat medium fine. Place the grated coconut in a bowl and pour hot milk over it. Marinate it for one hour, then drain through a fine cloth stretched over a bowl. Squeeze out the milk. You should have about one-and-a-half cups of coconut milk. Mix this with the reserved liquid drained from the coconut when you opened it.

Beat the egg yolks and sugar in a bowl until they are thick and lemon-colored. Add salt. Bring the coconut milk to a boil and stir a small part of it into the egg mixture. Over a low heat, add the egg mixture to the pan with the coconut milk and stir until the mixture thickens. Do not let it boil. Cool. Whip the cream until it soft peaks and combine with the coconut-egg mixture.

Freeze in an old-fashioned hand-turned freezer. Pour the ice cream mixture into the freezer, making sure that the freezer is cool. Fill the can not more than two-thirds full. Adjust the dasher and cover. Pack crushed ice and rock salt around the can, using six parts ice to one part salt. Turn the dasher slowly until the ice partially melts and forms brine. Add more ice and salt to maintain the ice level. Turn the handle constantly until the crank becomes hard to turn. Remove ice to below the lid of the can. Remove the lid and dasher.

To ripen the ice cream, plug the opening in the lid. Cover the can with several thicknesses of waxed paper. Make the covering as tight as possible. Replace the lid. Pack more ice and salt (use four parts ice to one part salt) around the can to fill the freezer. Cover the freezer with heavy cloth or croker sacks. Let the ice cream ripen for about four hours.

No matter what part of the South you live in, the hottest and clammiest weather is known as dog days. This uncomfortable season usually comes around the end of July and extends well into August.

Everybody knows that, in Alabama, dog days last forty days and during that time mockingbirds do not sing, a sore will not heal, and rattlesnakes are meaner than usual and will strike at anything that moves.

The only cure is to own a "mad stone." A mad stone, for those who don't know, is a hard, porous rock-like object found in the stomach of a deer. They are usually about the size of a quarter, smooth, and brown. If someone is bitten by a mad dog or a rattlesnake, he'll be safe if he owns a mad stone.

Southern Spicy Gingerbread

At Charity's picnic, the gingerbread was always served with fresh sliced peaches.

  2 fresh eggs
  3/4 cup brown sugar
  3/4 cup real molasses
  3/4 cup melted butter
  2 1/2 cups flour
  2 teaspoons ginger
  1 1/2 teaspoons cinnamon
  1/2 teaspoon cloves
  1/2 teaspoon nutmeg
  1/2 teaspoon baking powder
  1 cup boiling water

Preheat the oven to 350 degrees. Beat the eggs and add them to the sugar, molasses, and melted butter. Sift the dry ingredients and add them to the liquid mixture. Add the boiling water last. Bake in a shallow pan for approximately thirty minutes.

Charity's Rice Pudding

  2 1/2 cups cooked long-grain rice
  1/2 cup brown sugar
  1/2 cup light raisins
  1/4 cup top cream
  Dash grated nutmeg
  1 cup heavy whipping cream
  2 teaspoons strong coffee
  1/2 cup chopped pecans or walnuts

After cooking the rice, combine the hot rice with the brown sugar, raisins, top cream, nutmeg, and salt. Chill well. Just before serving, whip the cream with the coffee. Carefully fold the whipped cream and nuts into the rice mixture. This receipt serves around eight people.

Charity's Fried Chicken

There was always a controversy about Corrie's fried chicken versus Charity's fried chicken. Charity always steamed her chicken before frying it. She claimed the steam made the meat sweet and plump and besides, she figured, the chicken deserved to be steamed before its baptism by fire.

She would place a fryer, about two-and-a-half pounds, in a steamer and let it steam until done. Then she would follow her receipt.

1 2 1/2-pound fryer, steamed
2 teaspoons salt
Generous sprinkling freshly ground black pepper
1 egg, slightly beaten
1 1/2 cups buttermilk
Flour
Shortening for frying

Cut up the fryer in any way you desire. Sprinkle each piece with salt and pepper, then dip it into the buttermilk mixed with the egg. Roll each piece of chicken in flour and add another sprinkling of salt and pepper. The shortening (pure lard works best) has to be at least two inches deep in a heavy iron skillet. Have the shortening hot. Put the chicken in, one piece at a time. Do not crowd the pan. When the chicken is brown on one side, turn it over. Reduce the heat and cook for about fifteen minutes more. Drain on paper towels.

When you fry in deep fat, do not have the grease too hot.
A piece of bread should brown in forty counts—
that's a good temperature test.

Charity's Fresh Boiled Shrimp for Picnics

5 pounds large raw shrimp
3 quarts cold water
1/2 cup salt
3 1/2 teaspoons freshly ground black pepper
15 whole allspice
4 small onions, peeled and diced
4 bay leaves
1 bunch fresh celery, cut to first joint
Juice of 1 lemon
Rind of 1 lemon, grated
1 clove fresh garlic

Wash the shrimp well and drain. Combine all other ingredients in a large kettle. Bring to a boil and maintain for about three or four minutes. Put in the shrimp, cover the kettle, and boil slowly for fifteen to twenty minutes, depending on the size of the shrimp. When the shrimp are done, run cold water into the kettle till the shrimp sink to the bottom. Allow them to remain there for five minutes. Drain and spread the shrimp out to cool thoroughly. Peel and devein. Serve with fresh horseradish sauce (see page 83) or with any other sauce you prefer.

Shelby Springs Deviled Eggs by Charity

This receipt comes form a plantation day book, dated around 1887.

Shelby Springs was once a popular watering place for the wealthy plantation owners in Shelby County. It was first developed into a resort in 1839 for the marvelous medicinal properties of the springs. In 1855 the popularity of the resort intensified because the Tennessee and Alabama River Railroad was linked with the site. A fine two-story hotel was erected with a walkway leading to the railroad station. Cabins were built on the twenty-seven hundred acres of land.

During the Civil War, in 1862, the resort became a training ground for Confederate soldiers and was known as Camp Winn. In 1869 the area once again became a resort. The old hotel was destroyed by fire in 1881. A new one began operation in 1887, only to be destroyed by another fire in 1896. Rebuilding began with a building for dining and dancing and new cottages. In 1905 another new hotel opened; it was destroyed by fire in 1910. The resort closed forever in 1915.

The hotels at these famous watering places employed some of the most famous cooks from New Orleans and Mobile.

12 hard-boiled eggs
1/2 pint heavy cream
1/2 teaspoon dry mustard
1 teaspoon curry
1 tablespoon water
1 tablespoon mango chutney
Dash Tabasco
1/4 teaspoon honey

Whip the cream lightly. Mix the dry mustard with the water to make a paste. Add the curry powder. Combine this mixture with the whipped cream and add the chutney (you may substitute sweet pickle relish if you don't have chutney), Tabasco, and honey.

After hard-boiling the eggs, cool them as quickly as possible by plunging them into cold water. This will keep them from discoloring. Remove the shell and cut each egg in half lengthwise. Carefully remove the yolks, leaving the two halves of the white intact. Blend the filling with the removed yolks, and stuff the whites very full with the mixture. Top with a sprinkling of cayenne pepper.

Hard-Boiled Eggs

Be sure the eggs are fresh. If they tilt up on end or float in water, they are not fresh. Put the eggs in a saucepan and cover with lukewarm water (at least one-and-a-half inches over the eggs). Heat rapidly until the water boils. Take the pan off the stove, cover it tightly, and, leaving the same water in the saucepan, let it stand for fifteen minutes. Pour off the hot water and place the pan of eggs under cold running water. When the eggs are cool, hold each one under cold running water to peel.

Picnic Potato Salad

2 tablespoons vinegar
5 1/2 cups sliced cooked Irish potatoes
1 2/3 cups cucumbers, sliced
3/4 cup green peppers, chopped
4 tablespoons fresh onion, finely minced
1 1/2 cups fresh celery, chopped
3/4 pound cooked ham, chopped
1 cup salad dressing or mayonnaise
Sprinkling of freshly ground black pepper
1 teaspoon salt
1 teaspoon fresh chives, chopped

Pour the vinegar over the potatoes while they are still hot. Cool. Combine all the other ingredients and mix with the cooled potatoes. Chill for at least an hour before serving. This receipt will serve about ten people.

Charity's Picnic Potato Salad (*A Variation*)

2 1/2 cups sliced cooked potatoes
1 1/4 teaspoons salt
1 teaspoon sugar
1 1/2 teaspoons celery seed
1 teaspoon vinegar
1/2 cup onions, chopped, with a sprinkling of their green tops
3/4 cup mayonnaise
2 hard-boiled eggs, sliced
Fresh parsley

Sprinkle the potatoes with the seasonings and vinegar. Add the onion and, if you like, one-half cup chopped celery and one-quarter cup chopped sweet pickle. Add the mayonnaise and toss to mix. Chill well. Sprinkle the top with the sliced hard-boiled eggs and fresh parsley. This serves four people.

Picnic Watermelon for Adults Only

Plug a large, ripe snake watermelon by cutting a two-and-one-half-inch square about four inches deep. Pour about one pint of fine golden rum into the melon and replace the plug. Chill for about five hours.

Picnic Watermelon for Children

Cut the largest ripe snake watermelon you can find in half. The children will rip out the heart and eat it without any problems.

Meat Aspic Made by Charity on the Farm

Naturally there is a tale told about aspic. The name *aspic* suggests for some people the asp and, thus, gives this delicate jelly an unattractive connotation. The first aspics were made in the form of a coiled snake, and the tale hints that a certain small member of the asp family lies in wait for its prey in the bed of the transparent jelly, which he manufactures himself.

Napoleon Bonaparte's violent temper was as famous as the man himself. One story about that temper begins with a luncheon he planned for friends, who didn't show up. The emperor had to dine alone. The table was set with exquisite silver, fine porcelains, and gold plates. Displayed in the center of this splendor was a large, quivering, magnificent aspic, clear as glass, molded in the form of a coiled snake.

The emperor looked at the table and, in a moment of rage, turned it over, sending its contents crashing to the floor, including the aspic. His marshal took the news calmly. It was just another flare-up of Napoleon's temper. He summoned the chef, Dunand, and ordered him to set the dining room table exactly as it had been and told him to be sure to include the aspic!

This aspic is delicious plain; it also makes an excellent base for any type of aspic.

1 1/2 pounds veal bones
1 1/2 pounds beef bones
3 calves' feet
1/4 pound blanched fresh pork (rind and fat removed)
4 quarts water
1 tablespoon salt
2 fresh carrots, sliced
1 large onion
1 clove garlic
1 stalk celery

BOUQUET GARNI
Thyme
Parsley
Tarragon
Bay leaf

Put the first four ingredients in a soup kettle, cover the bones with the water, and bring to a boil. Remove ever particle of scum. Add the salt and simmer for four hours. Throw away the bones and meat and remove all fat from the surface of the liquid. Add the carrots, onion, garlic, celery, and bouquet garni. Return the soup kettle to the fire and simmer gently for another two hours. Strain and put into a bowl to cool. This makes about two-and-one-half quarts of clear, golden aspic.

REMINISCENCES OF A

Southern Christmas

Christmas Dinner Menu

Eggnog

Champagne

Fresh Oysters on the Half Shell

Fresh Horseradish Sauce

Roast Turkey with Apricot and Watermelon Rind

Preserves Divine

Lafayette Roasted Pecan Dressing

Loin of Fresh Pork

Green Apples Sautéed in Brandy

Mammoth Ripe Olives

Stuffed Green Olives

Baby Sweet Corn

Fresh Green Beans and Baby Carrots

Spoon Bread & Drop Biscuits

(Hot from the Butler's Pantry)

ON THE SIDEBOARD

Fig Preserves

Brandied Peaches

Strawberry Preserves (see page 137)

Sook's Famous Christmas Memory Fruitcake (see page 5)

Sook's Poinsettia Cake

Christmas Plum Pudding

Sugared Pecans with Orange

Dark Rum Orange Custard

Homemade Pulled Mints (see page 9)

Coffee

No holiday lays its warm hand on the individual heart as Christmas does. Then, as at no other season, we turn aside from the company of strangers to find the few who are close and dear and understanding. With them we renew the fire and color and rhythm of our lives.

This is why at Christmas we shun the crowd and fly away home. If there is in us some deep loneliness—and who has not some—all the year long we may keep up a bold heart among strangers and show a brave face to friends. But to be lonely at Christmas is to be lost indeed. Even the good friend can spare no more than a bright glance and a wave of the hand as he speeds past, homeward bound. Each must go to his own.

In the Faulk home, as with most, the heart of the house was the kitchen. It was always the same there in Monroeville at Christmas time. The huge black cast-iron stove was the center of attention. It made a happy roaring sound as it literally ate the fat lighter knots. Its ovens were full and the top eyes had pots and pans brimming with food for Christmas dinner.

On Christmas morning the smell of lard and hot cake batter was sweet in the kitchen. The breakfast hot cakes were eaten by the open fire, our only nourishment until Christmas dinner at three in the afternoon.

When the light switch was flipped on in the dining room that afternoon, we entered a place such as we might read about but had never imagined we would see. The table, a Chippendale with the banquet end on, seated twelve people comfortably. The tablecloth was softly glowing red satin, laid with delicate damask napkins and fine white china bordered by an inch of pure gold. The chandelier of a thousand shining eyes reflected the gleaming silver and crystal. We had everything from a twenty-five-pound turkey and wild strawberry preserves to Sook's fruitcake and poinsettia cake.

Each year as I slipped into my chair, my eyes took everything in. I received, as at no other time in my life, a sense of abundance, where nothing was stinted and cost was never considered.

Real Plantation Eggnog

This receipt was taken from the actual records of a farm journal dated 1846.

    12 egg yolks, beaten till light in color
    12 tablespoons powdered sugar
    12 tablespoons fine bourbon whiskey
    12 tablespoons fine Jamaican rum
    12 egg whites, stiffly beaten
    3 cups heavy cream, whipped

Beat the egg yolks until they are light, which requires a long beating time. Add the sugar and beat again until light. Add the whiskey and rum very, very slowly, beating all the time. Fold in the stiffly beaten egg whites and, lastly, fold in the whipped cream.

Serve in chilled silver cups with a sprinkling of fresh nutmeg on top.

Fresh Oysters on the Half Shell

Allow six oysters per person. To open, insert the blunt blade of an oyster knife between the shells and twist it to force them apart, cutting the large muscle close to the flat upper half of the shell. Throw away the flat shells and leave the oyster loose in the deeper shells. Serve with fresh horseradish sauce on a bed of shaved ice or finely chopped.

FRESH HORSERADISH SAUCE
Grate at least one pound of fresh horseradish root, peeled. Add one cup of breadcrumbs, moistened with a few teaspoons of milk, two tablespoons of sugar, one-and-one-half teaspoons dry mustard diluted with two tablespoons of vinegar, and a pinch of salt. Fold in

one cup of heavy cream, lightly whipped. Add freshly ground black pepper and chill.

The Cherokee Indians say heart trouble is caused by the lungs becoming wrapped around the heart and thus impeding its action. They believed that heart problems could be treated with a concoction of fern leaves because these leaves, when young, are coiled up, but they unwrap as they grow older.

Roast Turkey

Preheat the oven to 300 degrees. Clean a twenty-five-pound turkey thoroughly. Salt the inside of the bird. Fill the cavity with chopped tart apples, to be removed later and discarded. Rub the turkey all over with butter; then sprinkle it lightly with salt and flour. Put the turkey in a large brown paper bag. Roll the ends tightly and place the turkey on a roasting pan.

Do not open the bag to baste. Cook fifteen minutes per pound.

When the turkey is done, remove it from the oven and allow it to stand for about ten minutes. Cut the top off the bag and lift out the golden brown bird. In the bottom of the bag there will be plenty of rich stock, which can be diluted for gravy. Dressing should be baked separately, not stuffed in the bird, for this method of cooking.

Place the turkey on a very large footed silver tray and surround it with apricots in honey, crystallized fresh mint leaves (see page 155), and watermelon rind preserves.

Fresh Apricots in Mountain Sourwood Honey

20 fresh apricots
1 1/4 cups honey
1/4 cup fresh lemon juice
Dash fresh lemon rind, grated
1/2 cup kirsch

Peel about twenty fresh apricots. (Note: To peel fresh apricots, plunge them in boiling water for a few seconds, and the skins will slip off easily.) Remove the stones. Bring to a boil one-and-one-quarter cups of honey, one-quarter cup of fresh lemon juice, and a dash of grated fresh lemon rind. Add the apricot halves, reduce the heat, and simmer the fruit very gently for ten minutes or until tender. Do not break the apricots. Cool them in juice so they will plump up, then add one-half cup kirsch. Chill thoroughly. Place the apricots around the roasted turkey.

Watermelon Rind Preserves Divine

Thick, brittle rind
3/4 cup salt
1 tablespoon pulverized alum
1 heaping tablespoon slacked lime
1 1/4 pounds sugar per pound of rind
Lemon or ginger to flavor

Use a thick, brittle rind and pull all green from the outside and all pink from the inside. Cut the rind into any shape you desire.

Prepare the rind in the afternoon in a vessel large enough so that the pieces are covered with water. Sprinkle three-quarters of a cup of salt in the water and soak overnight.

Early the next morning, pour off the salt water, rinse the rind in clear water, and cover again with water, this time adding a tablespoon of pulverized alum, mixing it thoroughly all through the water. Let the rind soak in this solution for two hours.

Rinse the rind again and fill the vessel with clear water. Dissolve one heaping tablespoon of slacked lime in a pint of water, stir well, and let the solution settle. Pour the lime water, after it settles, over the rinds and soak for two hours. Then rinse the rinds and put them on the stove with enough water to cover them.

Boil them until you can pierce them with a fork or straw. When they are tender, drain off all the water and weigh the rinds. Allow one-and-one-quarter pounds of sugar per pound of rinds. Put them on the stove; add the sugar and enough water to cover them. Use lemon or ginger to flavor the rinds. Boil them until the rinds turn a creamy yellow and the syrup is thick. Put the preserves in jars, cover with syrup, and seal.

When preserves turn to sugar after you make them, it is because you did not put enough water in after putting in the sugar. It takes longer boiling, but it pays off in the long run. Boil for two-and-a-half or three hours.

Lafayette Roasted Pecan Dressing

This is the dressing served to Lafayette when he visited Claiborne, Alabama, in 1825.

1 turkey liver, mashed fine
14 slices homemade bread, toasted
4 tablespoons pure lard
1/2 cup fresh butter
1 teaspoon salt
1 teaspoon freshly ground black pepper
1/2 teaspoon freshly ground nutmeg
1 tablespoon fresh thyme
1 tablespoon fresh parsley, chopped
1/2 teaspoon fresh sage
Pan of boiling water
1 cup slivered almonds
6 hard-boiled eggs
1/2 teaspoon freshly ground mace
2 1/2 cups salted, roasted pecans, chopped fine
1 large onion
1/2 cup sherry
2 tablespoons lard
1/2 cup fresh celery, chopped fine
1 small fresh green pepper, chopped fine

The turkey liver should be cold. Crumble it up in a large bowl and add the butter, salt, lard, fresh celery, black pepper, thyme, grated nutmeg, crumbled bread, sage, green pepper, and parsley. Pour in a little boiling water and mix well by hand. Add the whites of the hard-boiled eggs and the yolks that have been mixed with the mace. Then add the slivered almonds, salted pecans, and sherry. Mix thoroughly. Put the onion, grated or finely cut, into a frying pan with the lard and fry until brown. Allow to cool and then mix thoroughly with the other ingredients. This will stuff a twenty-five-pound turkey.

To peel pecans easily, cover them with boiling water for a few minutes, drain, and crack them on the ends. The sides will break and the meats will come out in halves.

Loin of Fresh Pork

1 large loin of fresh pork
2 tablespoons salt
1 tablespoon black pepper
1 teaspoon nutmeg
1/2 teaspoon fresh sage
Claret
1/4 cup bacon fat
3 cloves cut fresh garlic
1/2 cup fresh parsley, chopped
Bouquet Garni
2 cups beef stock

BOUQUET GARNI
1 large bay leaf
1 sprig fresh thyme
2 sprigs fresh celery leaves
Small amount fresh horseradish root

Preheat the oven the 375 degrees. Rub the pork well on all sides with the salt, pepper, nutmeg, and sage. Sear it in the bacon fat, heated with the garlic and parsley. Put the pork in a baking pan. Add the bouquet garni tied up with a heavy white thread. Cover with claret and bake, allowing thirty to thirty-five minutes per pound. Turn the pork occasionally as it roasts. When the meat is done, the wine should have evaporated.

Remove the meat and pour the beef stock into the roasting pan. Brown some flour and mix it with a little stock. Pour this remaining roux into the stock and heat until it boils. Garnish with slices of green apples browned in burnt sugar and brandy.

Baby Sweet Corn

These ears of corn are canned in jars and saved for the holidays and special occasions. They are picked when they are about five inches long. Allow four per person.

48 ears baby corn
2 cups fresh butter
Salt
Fresh ground white pepper
1/3 cup each chopped fresh parsley, chives, and chervil

Drain the corn and soak it in water for one hour. Be sure the corn is covered. Drain.

Heat salted water in a saucepan over high heat until it boils. Add the corn and cover. Let the corn stand, off the heat, for five minutes. Drain thoroughly and top with butter, parsley, chives, and chervil and a dusting of the white pepper.

Fresh Green Beans and Baby Carrots

4 pounds fresh tender string beans
4 pounds baby carrots, trimmed and pared
8 tablespoons fresh butter
8 tablespoons fresh parsley, minced
Salt
Freshly ground black pepper

Cook the beans in boiling water for about seven minutes until they are crisp and tender. Drain thoroughly. Add the carrots to the same boiling water and cook for ten minutes. Melt the butter in a skillet over low heat and add the vegetables. Sprinkle with parsley, and add salt and pepper.

Fresh Water-Ground Spoon Bread

1 cup freshly ground cornmeal
1 cup boiling water
3 eggs
1 teaspoon salt
1/3 cup melted butter
1 1/2 cups sweet milk
3 teaspoons baking powder

Preheat the oven to 375 degrees. Pour the boiling water over the cornmeal. Stir to prevent lumping. Beat the eggs until they are frothy and put them into the milk along with the salt and baking powder. Add the liquid slowly to the meal mixture. Mix in the melted butter. Pour the mixture into a well-greased deep iron skillet and bake for a little more than a half-hour. Serve piping hot.

Old-Fashioned Drop Biscuits

2 cups sifted flour
1 teaspoon salt
1 teaspoon baking powder
2 well-beaten fresh eggs
3/4 cup heavy cream

Preheat the oven 375 degrees. Sift all the dry ingredients together. Add the eggs and heavy cream. Stir for a short time. The dough should be soft and lumpy. Use a table-spoon to drop dough onto a greased baking sheet. Bake for about fifteen minutes. This makes about a half-dozen large biscuits.

Old-Timey Fig Preserves

Truman once said, "Remember, a fig tree will not grow in a lonely place. It has to be planted by a well-worn path."

>   5 pounds figs
>   3 pounds sugar
>   Lemon or ginger to flavor

Put just enough water into the sugar to wet it. Put the sugar over a fire and melt it. Boil until a rather thick syrup is produced. Put in half the figs. Boil slowly until the mixture is pink and the syrup is thick. Stir to prevent sticking. When the figs look pink and clear, lift them out onto a platter and place them in the sun. Put in the other half of the figs and cook in the same way. When the second lot of figs is done and the syrup is thick, pack the fruit in jars, fill with the boiling syrup, and seal.

Place the first lot cooked into the boiling syrup that remains, and bring this to a boil just long enough to heat the figs through. Place the fruit in jars, cover with syrup, and seal.

You can cook lemon or ginger in with the figs if you like the taste. If you prefer lemon, add one or more lemons cut in thin slices. For a ginger flavor, cook four or five pieces of ginger in with the figs.

Figs cooked in small lots float and are not so apt to burn. They also retain their shape better. The cooking must be slow and the stirring done carefully so as not to break the fruit. Ripe, firm figs with the stems on are the best for preserving.

Southern Brandied Peaches

>   Fresh yellow freestone peaches
>   Sugar
>   Brandy
>   1/4 pound soda
>   Water to match sugar, cup for cup

Add the soda to a pail of water. When it comes to a rolling boil, throw in two or three peaches at a time. Let them remain for about five minutes, throw them into cold water for a minute, then rub the fuzz and skin off with a linen towel. After this, throw them into another pail of cold water until all the peaches have been prepared. Make a syrup while the peaches are being prepared, using three-quarters of a pound of sugar to each pound of fruit, with one cup of water for each cup of sugar. When the syrup comes to a boil, add the peaches and boil until they can be easily pierced with a fork. Pack into jars, filling half with syrup from the peaches and half with brandy. A two-inch stick of cinnamon may be added to each jar, if you desire.

Poinsettia Cake

Most Christmas greenery reflects European traditions: kissing-ring mistletoe, boughs of holly, Luther's tiny pine. But one colorful plant—the flaming star-like poinsettia—is a native of this continent. First introduced to this country in 1828 by Dr. Joel Robert Poinsett, our first minister to Mexico, the plant now bears his name. The people of Mexico and Central America call this brilliant tropical plant *flor de la Noche Buena,* which translates, "flower of the Holy Night."

A wonderful Mexican legend explains the plant's origin. An orphan boy, having finished running his errands, sadly counted his centavos. The young boy, named Pedro, realized that he hardly had enough to buy his evening meal.

"Come with us to the cathedral," urged his friends.

"No, I have no money to buy a gift for the Christ child," he answered.

"Take this," suggested one of his friends, pointing to a weed by the side of the road.

Hesitantly, Pedro reached down and picked the stringy weed, climbed the steep hill to the church, and slowly made his way to the altar with its *nacimiento* (a Mexican nativity scene). Kneeling, he reverently laid his gift in front of the figure of the Christ Child.

He soon became aware of the commotion of the crowed. In wide-eyed amazement he saw a dazzling and beautiful scarlet flower where only dried leaves and stems had existed only a moment ago. His humble offering had been miraculously transformed into something truly beautiful.

1 cup pure butter

3 cups sugar

4 cups flour

2 rounded teaspoons baking powder

1 cup whole milk

Pure vanilla (to taste)

Red vegetable coloring

10 egg whites, stiffly beaten

Preheat the oven to 350 degrees. Cream the butter and sugar until they are fluffy. Sift the flour two times and gradually fold it into the butter-sugar mixture, adding the milk, then the egg whites, and, lastly, the baking powder, vanilla, and enough red coloring to make the batter a Christmas red.

Be very careful when folding in the egg whites. Do not beat them into the batter.

Pour the batter into pans that have been lined with waxed paper and bake for twenty-five to thirty minutes.

FROSTING

1 cup sugar

2 egg whites

3 tablespoons water

1 teaspoon pure vanilla

1/4 teaspoon cream of tartar

Pinch salt

Put all the ingredients in the top of a double boiler, with water already boiling in the lower half. Beat constantly with an egg beater for seven minutes. Remove from the heat and spread on the cooled cake, inside and out. Sprinkle freshly grated coconut inside and on the top and sides of the cake.

DECORATING ICING

1 cup confectioners' sugar

1 egg white, unbeaten

1 teaspoon cream of tartar

1/4 teaspoon pure almond flavoring

Beat one cup of confectioners' sugar into one unbeaten egg white. Beat until the icing stands in peaks. Add one teaspoon of cream of tartar, coloring if desired, and one-quarter teaspoon of pure almond flavoring. If the icing doesn't thicken, add a little more confectioners' sugar.

MAKING THE POINSETTIAS

Tint the decorating icing a bright red. After icing the cake and sprinkling the coconut on top, place a slice from a cupcake on the back of the cake so that the poinsettias will be slightly elevated. This is where you will place the first one.

Years ago only parchment cones were used for decorating cakes. Now, however, the muslin oil-proof bags that are available are acceptable as well.

The petals of the poinsettia are made with a leaf tube, size 70. Fill the cone about two-thirds full and fold over the top. Making the poinsettia requires a quick, dexterous motion.

The leaves are large and radiate from a center about as large as a quarter. Place the tube on top of the coconut icing and press out the first petal. Press hard so that the base of the petal will be thick. Still pressing, raise the tube up and away in a very quick motion so the petal will stand erect. If you move slowly, the petal will not stand up.

There is no set rule about the number of leaves you will make. Make the cake look luxurious. Be sure all the petals radiate from a common center.

The background leaves of the poinsettia are made with the same tube, only using green icing instead of red. Press out the leaves behind the poinsettia, not too close, so that you can put in some bunches of holly.

After you finish making as many poinsettias as you like, put the finishing touches on. With tube number 3, press out a number of dots to form the center of the plant, about the size of a small pea. Tint the icing a pale green. Take the number 2 tube and put a dot in bright yellow on top of the green. Last, touch each bright yellow dot with a tinier dot of red from a number 3 tube.

The holly leaves are a dark, rich green. Use tube number 70 to press out a cluster of holly and on top of the leaves, with tube number 3, arrange holly berries in groups of five, six, or seven.

When this cake is completed, the poinsettias should cover the top and drape over the sides with the holly in between the flowers.

Christmas Plum Pudding

It is a mystery why plum pudding is called *plum pudding* because it is made without plums. It was once made with prunes, which are dried plums, and it was originally called plum porridge. It stems from a dish known as "frumenty," which at one time was Christmas fare in many parts of England. Later, spices and prunes or plums were added, the latter eventually being supplanted by raisins. By the end of the seventeenth century, it had become a proper steamed pudding, rich with fruits and spices. But the name *plum* stuck, and does to this day.

2 pounds currants
2 pounds raisins
1/2 pound each citron, almonds, and red cherries
1 pound brown sugar
1 pound flour, browned
1 pound sweet butter
1/2 pound dry breadcrumbs
1 cup molasses
1/2 cup strong coffee
1/2 cup grape juice
2 teaspoons soda
1 teaspoon baking powder
1 teaspoon cinnamon
1 teaspoon allspice
1 grated nutmeg
1/2 teaspoon cloves
7 eggs

Cut the citron, cherries, and almonds, mix the spices, baking powder, and soda with flour, and dredge the fruit in this mixture. Cream the butter and sugar, beat the eggs lightly, and add them to the butter and sugar. Add the molasses and other liquids, mixing thoroughly with the fruit. Fill one-pound coffee cans, well-greased, half full and steam for three hours by placing the cans on a rack in boiling water. Keep the water three-quarters deep on the cans. Replenish as necessary.

When the pudding is ready to serve, place it on a platter to set before the hostess. Saturate lumps of loaf sugar with pure lemon extract and place this sugar around and over the pudding. Light the sugar mixture with a match, and beautiful blue flames will leap from the burning extract and sugar until the extract is consumed.

Be sure to have everything ready when the extract is poured and lighted so the burning flames may be effective. This extract must be lemon to burn. This lighted pudding was much used in olden times.

You can also flame the dessert by turning the hot steamed pudding onto your handsomest silver platter and spooning warmed aged brandy over it, two or three tablespoons. Light with a match and top with a sprig of fresh holly just before carrying it to the table.

In Britain, plum pudding is traditionally made in a large, buttered ceramic mixing bowl and is steamed for six hours. Some receipts call for two to three weeks of ripening before serving.

Sugared Pecans with Orange

1 cup sugar
1/4 teaspoon salt
2 teaspoons grated orange rind
6 tablespoons rich milk
1/2 teaspoon pure vanilla
3 cups freshly shelled pecan halves

Combine the sugar, salt, milk, and fresh grated orange rind in a large heavy saucepan. Cook until the mixture reaches the soft-ball stage, about 258 degrees, stirring often.

Remove from the heat and add the vanilla, then the nuts. Stir until grainy and all the pecans are coated. Turn out on waxed paper. Be sure and separate the nuts. Cool and age in an airtight container for several days.

Dark Rum Orange Custard

3 cups fresh orange juice
12 eggs, well beaten
3/4 cup powdered sugar
3/4 cup dark rum
2 tablespoons grated orange peel
1 1/2 cups heavy cream, whipped

Preheat the oven to about 350 degrees. Mix the sugar and the orange juice and stir until the sugar is dissolved. Blend in the dark rum and eggs. Pour into individual ramekins and bake in a shallow pan filled with water. Test by inserting a broom straw in the center. If it comes out clean, the custards are done. Chill for several hours and serve with whipped cream and grated orange peel.

Cook cup custards on a trivet placed in hot water or on many folds of paper. The custard will then be firm and smooth and will not curdle or whey.

RECEIPTS FROM

Plantation Farm Ledgers, Day Books, and Journals

Dating as Far Back as 1837

Real Strawberry Shortcake

Ever since the days when the colonists first discovered the juicy good-
ness of strawberries, the shortcake has been a favorite. Originally, the
berries went to market strung on straw and, thus, the name.

4 cups flour
1/4 cup sugar
6 teaspoons baking powder
1 teaspoon salt
1 cup fresh butter
2 eggs, well-beaten
1 1/3 cups pure top cream
4 cups strawberries, sliced and sweetened
1 cup extra heavy whipping cream

Preheat the oven to 450 degrees. Sift together the sugar, flour, baking
powder, and salt. Cut in the butter till the mixture resembles small
peas. Combine the eggs and the top cream and add all at once to the
dry ingredients, stirring just enough to moisten. Spread the dough in
two greased round cake tins, building up the edges slightly so that the
shortcake will not hump in the middle. Bake for about eighteen minutes. Butter the top of one layer. Remove from the pans and cool.

Whip the whipping cream and spoon half the strawberries and
whipped cream over the buttered layer. Add the top layer and top
with the remaining cream and strawberries.

Old-Fashioned Kiss Pudding

6 egg whites
2 cups sugar
Pinch salt
1 tablespoon vinegar
1 teaspoon pure vanilla extract

Beat the egg whites dry and gently fold in the sugar, a small amount at a time. Add the salt, vinegar, and vanilla and mix well. Pour the mixture into a well-greased pan. Place the pan in a cold oven and then turn the heat to 300 degrees. Bake about thirty minutes. Cut into serving pieces and top with any fresh fruit that is in season.

Ham Bone and Snap Beans

After the first snap beans are picked and snapped, the ends of the strings should be thrown on the top of the house so that the vines will grow very tall, as tall as the house, and bear abundantly.

3 pounds of fresh snap beans
Salt to taste
1 bone from a cooked ham
Small amount of red pepper
1 teaspoon summer savory, chopped fine

Wash, snap, and string the beans. Place the ham bone in a large iron kettle, cover well with water, and let this simmer for one hour. Add the snap beans and the seasonings, except the savory, and cook until the beans are tender and the meat from the ham bone has flavored them. Sprinkle the fresh savory over the top of the cooked beans just before serving them. Serve with homemade cornbread.

Country Fried Corn

10 ears fresh yellow corn
1/2 cup milk

3/4 teaspoon salt

1/4 teaspoon black pepper

6 tablespoons pure butter

1/4 teaspoon fresh thyme, minced fine

Cut the corn from the cob and add the milk, pepper, and salt. Melt the butter in a skillet and add the corn mixture. Add the thyme. Cook, stirring, until tender. Some cooks add two eggs to the mixture just before taking the corn from the skillet.

Baked Beans and Brown Bread

According to the plantation day book, baked beans had their start with the Pilgrims. It seems that cooking was forbidden on the Sabbath. The beans and the brown bread were baked the night before, then heated to piping hot the next day.

2 cups dry navy beans

1/2 teaspoon salt

1/3 cup brown sugar

4 ounces salt pork

2 quarts cold water

1/2 cup molasses

1 teaspoon dry mustard

1 medium onion, chopped

Rinse the beans and add them to the water in a heavy iron pot. Bring them to a boil, then simmer for two minutes. Remove them from the heat. Cover and let them stand for at least one hour; they can stand overnight. Drain, reserving liquid.

Preheat the oven to 300 degrees. Measure two cups of the liquid, adding more water if needed, and mix it with the molasses, brown sugar, and mustard. Cut the salt pork in half and score one half. Thinly slice the remaining pork.

In a two-quart bean pot combine the beans, onions, and thinly sliced pork. Pour the molasses mixture over the beans. Top with the scored pork. Cover and bake five to seven hours. Add more liquid if needed. This receipt will serve about ten people.

Boston Brown Bread

1 cup all-purpose flour
1 teaspoon baking powder
1 teaspoon soda
1 teaspoon salt
1 cup cornmeal
1 cup whole wheat flour
2 cups buttermilk
1 cup raisins
3/4 cup molasses

Sift together all-purpose flour, baking powder, soda, and salt. Stir in cornmeal and whole wheat flour. Add buttermilk, raisins, and molasses. Beat well.

Divide the batter into four portions. Grease and flour four large fruit cans. After putting one-fourth of the batter in each can, cover the end with brown paper and secure. Place on a rack in a deep iron kettle. Add boiling water to a depth of about one inch. Cover and steam three hours, adding more boiling water if necessary. Uncover the cans and cool for ten minutes. Remove the bread. Wrap in brown paper and store overnight.

Date Muffins

1 3/4 cups all-purpose flour
1/4 cup sugar
2 1/2 teaspoons baking powder
3/4 teaspoon salt
1 egg, well beaten
3/4 cup milk
1/3 cup butter, melted
3/4 cup dates, coarsely snipped.

Preheat the oven to 400 degrees. Sift the flour, baking powder, sugar, and salt into a bowl. Combine the milk, egg, and butter. Add all at once to the dry ingredients. Stir until barely moist. Gently stir in the dates. Bake in a greased muffin pan for twenty-five minutes. This receipt will make about twelve muffins.

Old Slave Molasses Pie

1 cup sugar
1 tablespoon butter, softened
2 cups molasses
3 fresh eggs
Juice of 1 fresh lemon
Ground nutmeg
1 unbaked 9-inch pie shell

Preheat the oven to 350 degrees. Mix the sugar and butter together well. Add the molasses. Beat the eggs until they are fluffy. Stir in the molasses mixture and add the lemon juice. Mix well and pour into the unbaked pie shell. Sprinkle nutmeg lightly over the top. Bake about forty-five minutes or until a broom straw inserted in the middle comes out clean.

Pork Roasted with Coarse Salt

7- or 8-pound loin of fresh pork
12 bay leaves (more if needed)
Coarse salt (sea salt or ice cream salt)
Peppercorns
1 cup ice water
1 cup black currant jam

Preheat the oven to 500 degrees. Cut slits the length of the pork roast at even intervals on the fat side of the loin. In each slit insert a bay leaf and about two peppercorns per slit. Pour the coarse salt heavily over the entire roast and put in on a rack in a roasting pan. Put the roast in the hot oven for five minutes, then lower the heat to 350 degrees and roast for thirty minutes per pound.

Thirty minutes before the roast is done, pour the ice water over it and, after a few minutes, spread the black currant jam over the entire surface. Baste two or three times during the remaining cooking period.

This makes a handsome roast with an outer crust of coarse salt overlaid by black currants.

Ginger and White Pepper Lemon Cake

When I found this receipt in a plantation farm journal dated 1849, I could not believe it. It seemed too improbable that pepper would be used in a cake. It is delicious! This cake will keep for several days, but some of the hot, spicy taste fades gradually. It is best eaten at once, sliced paper-thin.

> Grated rind of 2 large lemons
> 2 1/2 tablespoons fresh lemon juice
> 3 cups all-purpose flour, well sifted
> 1/2 ounce fresh ginger
> 3/4 teaspoon baking soda
> 3/4 teaspoon double-acting baking powder
> 2 teaspoons fresh ground white pepper
> 1/2 teaspoon salt
> 8 ounces unsalted butter
> 1 3/4 cups granulated sugar
> 3 large fresh eggs
> 1 cup buttermilk

Preheat the oven to 325 degrees. Bake in a tube pan with a decorated bottom if you have one.

In a small bowl, mix the lemon rind, lemon juice, and ground ginger. Sift together the baking soda, baking powder, flour, salt, and white pepper, and set aside.

In another bowl, beat the butter until it is soft, add the sugar, and beat for another two minutes. Add the eggs, one at a time, until they are blended with other ingredients. Gradually add the sifted dry ingredients along with the buttermilk. Mix in the lemon and the ginger mixture.

The batter will be heavy, so shake the pan to level the cake out before baking. Bake for about one hour (maybe a little longer) or until a broom straw inserted in the middle comes out clean.

GLAZE FOR THE CAKE

1/2 cup fresh lemon juice
3/4 cup granulated sugar

When the cake is removed from the oven and the pan, stir the ingredients together to form the glaze. With a brush, cover the entire cake, even the hole. The hot cake will absorb the glaze.

Clouted Cream

TAKEN FROM A SELMA PLANTATION LEDGER, DATED 1843

4 blades mace
1 gill fresh milk
6 teaspoons rose water
2 egg yolks, well beaten
1 quart very heavy cream

String the mace on a piece of sewing thread. Put this thread into the fresh milk (a gill equals one-quarter pint) and rose water. Simmer for a few minutes. Then by degrees add this liquid, strained, into the egg yolks. Stir the whole mixture into the heavy cream and set it over the fire. Stir it till the mixture is hot but not boiling.

When the cream is done, a round mark about the size of the bottom of the pan it is in will appear on the surface. In the Deep South this mark is called the "ring." When it is seen, remove the cream from the heat.

Pour it into a deep dish and let stand for twenty-four hours. Serve it in a deep cream dish to eat with fresh fruits, especially blackberries, dewberries, and strawberries.

Cat's Tongues

TAKEN FROM AN 1841 PLANTATION LEDGER

1/4 pint heavy cream
7 ounces caster (powdered) sugar
2 drops pure vanilla extract
8 ounces sifted flour
6 egg whites

Preheat the oven to 425 degrees. Whip the cream until it is stiff. Add the sugar and the vanilla. Fold in the flour. Beat the egg whites until they are very stiff and fold them into the mixture. Lightly grease a baking tray. Either pipe the mixture onto the pan or use a parchment piping bag. Leave at least one inch between each one as they spread when they are baking. Bake in a hot oven until there is a fringe of brown around the edge. When completely cool, these can be stored in an airtight container.

Whiskey and Honey Sauce

1/4 pint very heavy cream
1/4 pint honey
2 tablespoons fine bourbon whiskey

Heat the cream and the honey over a very slow heat. Add the bourbon and blend well. This should be served hot.

Fresh Lemon Posset

TAKEN FROM AN 1841 PLANTATION DAY BOOK

At first possets were made with cream, not milk, sugar, and nutmeg, curdled with a pint of sack, or ale. Frequently, thickening was effected by pouring the hot mixture over small pieces of bread. They were served hot in winter, but in summer the curdled mixture was allowed to cool to the consistency of a junket and the surplus wine or ale was drawn off. In the eighteenth century, milk was substituted for cream. The posset was always eaten with a spoon. Shakespeare, in his *Merry Wives of Windsor,* writes, "Yet be cheerful, Knight; thou shalt eat a posset to-night in my house."

2 fresh lemons
4 ounces fine sugar
1/4 pint dry white wine
4 egg whites
1 pint extra heavy cream

Pare the rind from one lemon and slice it very thinly and set aside. Grate the rind of the other lemon. Squeeze the juice from both lemons into a bowl, adding the sugar, wine, and grated lemon rind. Let it stand for half an hour so that the flavors can blend. Beat the egg whites until peaks are formed. Add the cream to the wine, sugar, and lemon mixture and beat until it is stiff. Fold in the egg white very carefully. Chill well before serving. Decorate with the thinly sliced lemon rind.

Old-Timey Paper-Bag Apple Pie

This method was used in the 1800s to bake pies. It is the same method used to roast a turkey (see page 84).

FILLING
2 1/2 pounds tart cooking apples, peeled, cored, and chunked
2 tablespoons fresh lemon juice with 1 teaspoon thyme mixed in
1/2 cup sugar
2 tablespoons unsifted all-purpose flour
1/2 teaspoon ground cinnamon
Dash ground nutmeg

PASTRY
1 1/2 cups unsifted all-purpose flour
1/2 teaspoon salt
1/3 cup (rounded) shortening
5 or 6 tablespoons ice water

TOPPING
1/2 cup unsifted all-purpose flour
1/2 cup pure butter
1/4 cup sugar
1/4 cup brown sugar, firmly packed

In a large bowl toss the apples with the lemon juice and thyme. In a small bowl combine the sugar, flour, cinnamon, and nutmeg for the filling. Sprinkle this mixture over the apples and toss until they are well coated. Set them aside while preparing the pastry.

In a bowl combine the flour and salt for the pastry. With two knives used scissor-fashion, cut in the shortening until the mixture resembles coarse crumbs. Gradually add ice water and stir with a fork until the flour is moistened and the pastry leaves the side of the bowl. Shape the pastry into a ball. On a lightly floured surface, roll the pastry into a twelve-inch circle. Line a nine-inch pie tin with the pastry. Make a high fluted edge to hold in the apple juices. Spoon the apples into the pastry.

Preheat the oven to 400 degrees. In a small bowl combine the topping ingredients and stir until a smooth paste is formed. Gently dollop the paste over the apples, then spread the topping to cover the pie.

Place the pie in a large brown paper bag and close the open end with paper clips or sew it together. Place the bag on an oven rack in the center of the oven. Be sure the bag does not touch the bottom, sides, or top of the oven. Bake for about one hour. Remove the pie from the oven but do not open the bag. Let the pie cool inside the bag on a wire rack for ten minutes. Carefully cut the bag open and remove the pie. Serve it warm. This receipt makes about eight servings.

Molasses Pie

According to an old superstition in the South, it is fitting and proper to save the pointed tip of a wedge of pie for the last bite. A wish will come true if the top of the pie is cut off, pushed to the side of the plate, and eaten last. Also, the wish must be repeated silently just before the last bite is taken, and not a word must be spoken until everyone has left the dining table.

    1 cup brown sugar
    1/2 cup molasses
    1 1/2 tablespoons flour
    2 1/2 tablespoons butter, melted
    3 eggs, well beaten
    Pinch salt
    1/2 cup black walnuts
    1 9-inch unbaked pie shell

Preheat the oven to 450 degrees. Mix all the ingredients together and pour them into the pie shell. Bake for ten minutes. Reduce the heat to 325 degrees and bake for thirty minutes more or until a broom straw inserted into the middle comes out clean.

Beaten Biscuits

Beaten biscuits are an old tradition in the Deep South. The dough for these little biscuits is actually beaten with a mallet, hammer, or even an ax, which was the instrument used by women during the Civil War when they had nothing else to work with, for anywhere from twenty-five to fifty minutes or until the dough pops like a shot.

This receipt, according to Corrie, is from a sugar plantation in New Orleans. It is a well-known fact that Creole ladies were very frugal and oftentimes sent their own servants onto the streets of the city to sell delicacies from home gardens and kitchens. Beaten biscuits were a great favorite for this commercial enterprise.

  1 teaspoon butter, softened
  2 cups flour
  1 1/2 teaspoon sugar
  1 teaspoon salt
  2 tablespoons hog lard
  1/4 cup milk mixed with 1/4 cup water

Preheat the oven to 400 degrees. Spread the butter evenly over the bottom of the baking pan and set aside.

Sift the flour, salt, and sugar together at least twice. Mix the lard (fingers are best for this) with the dry ingredients until the mixture is mealy. Add the milk to form a stiff dough.

Place the dough on a floured surface and keep folding it and beating it (the age-old rule is two hundred times for homefolks and four hundred for high company) until blisters appear on the dough.

Roll the dough to a thickness of about one-third of an inch and cut with a small cutter (a little larger than a thimble). Pierce the top of each biscuit with the tines of a silver fork to make a design. Bake in a hot oven for fifteen to twenty minutes.

The biscuits will keep for a week or more if stored in tightly closed box.

Plantation Ginger Cookies

1 cup dry bread crumbs
1/2 cup brown sugar
1/8 teaspoon salt
1 teaspoon ginger
1/2 teaspoon soda
2 eggs, beaten
1 teaspoon butter, melted
1 teaspoon pure vanilla
1/4 cup molasses

Preheat the oven to 400 degrees. Combine the dry ingredients, add the beaten eggs, butter, and molasses. From a spoon, drop the cookies about two inches apart onto a buttered baking pan. Bake for about fifteen minutes.

Fresh Raspberry Fool

1 quart fresh raspberries
1 1/2 cups clotted cream

Mash raspberries thoroughly through a fine sieve and sweeten to taste. Combine the crushed berries with the clotted cream (heavy cream that has been allowed to sour slightly). More sugar can be added if needed. Serve in very thin all-crystal glasses that have been chilled. Serve with sugar wafers.

Lemon Custard Pie

6 eggs, well beaten
1 1/2 cups sugar
2/3 cup freshly squeezed lemon juice
1 1/2 tablespoons grated lemon rind
1 1/2 cups water
1 unbaked 9-inch pie shell
Nutmeg

Preheat the oven to 425 degrees. Mix thoroughly all the ingredients in a large bowl. Pour them into the pie shell and bake for twenty-five minutes. Lower the temperature to 275 degrees and bake for about ten minutes longer. Cool on a rack so that the bottom will not be soggy. Sprinkle a little freshly ground nutmeg over the top.

Tallahassee Hush Puppies

This receipt comes from an elderly black man in Tallahassee, Florida, and it comes with an interesting story.

Years ago the blacks of Tallahassee would get together on warm fall evenings for a sugar cane grinding. Someone in the crowd would feed the sugar cane into a one-mule treadmill while another poured the juice into a large kettle where it was boiled to sugar. After their work was completed, they would gather around the open fire, over which was hung an iron pot in which fish and corn pones were cooked in fresh lard.

The little corn pones were delicious and appetizing. While the food was sizzling in the grease, the people waiting would start up a weird conversation, binding each other in a spell of tall stories about haints, panthers, and bear hunts. On the outer edge of the circle of light reflected by the fire would sit their hound dogs, their ears alert for strange noises and their noses raised to catch a whiff of the savory odor of the frying fish and sizzling corn pones.

When the talk ceased for a moment, a low whine of hunger from the dogs would attract the attention of the men, and, without thinking, one of them would reach for some of the corn pone that had been placed on a tree stump to cool. The generous donor would break off a piece of the pone and toss it to the hungry dogs with the muffled murmur of "Hush, puppy!"

    2 cups fresh-ground cornmeal
    2 teaspoons homemade baking powder
    1 teaspoon salt
    1 1/2 cups sweet milk
    1/2 cup water
    1 large onion, chopped fine

Stir the dry ingredients together and add the milk and water. Stir in the chopped onion. Add more meal or milk as necessary to form a soft dough, but one stiff enough to be workable. With the hands, mold pieces of the dough into small pones, about five inches long, three inches wide, and three-quarters of an inch thick. Fry in deep fat until well browned.

The expression "Fingers were made before forks" originated with the English. They held the fork in great contempt. Today, we take forks for granted, but they were seldom seen on dining tables three hundred years ago. Until the early eighteenth century, almost the whole population in France, England, and America (from the lofty to the lowly) ate with their fingers or used the tip of a knife to convey food to the mouth.

Aunt Phronie's Pumpkin Pie

To bake a pumpkin for a pie, wash it and cut the pumpkin in half crosswise. Scrape out the seeds and stringy parts. Place the halves in a dripping pan, shell side up, and bake until they begin to fall apart and are tender. Scrape the pulp from the shell and strain it.

1 cup fresh strained pumpkin
1/4 cup sugar
1/2 teaspoon salt
1/4 teaspoon mace
1/4 teaspoon cinnamon
1/2 teaspoon pure vanilla
1/2 teaspoon cloves
1/4 teaspoon ginger
2 beaten eggs
1/2 cup whole milk
1/2 cup pure cream
1 9-inch unbaked pie shell

Preheat the oven to 475 degrees. Mix the dry ingredients. Add the pumpkin, eggs, milk, and cream gradually. Pour the mixture into a pie plate lined with the unbaked crust. Bake for fifteen minutes in the hot oven, then for twenty-five minutes with the heat reduced to a moderate temperature (350 degrees).

Fresh Peach Fritters

In the South fresh peaches are used for preserves, pickles, marmalade, peach conserve, and just plain eating. But the peach tree serves another purpose. Any child born in the South can remember the keen switches provided for punishing errant children. A peach switch really nettled and stung bare legs. All this could be endured, however, by thinking back to fresh sliced peaches in lakes of thick cream and the tiny animals carved from the peach pits by a loving uncle or grandfather.

Oil for frying
1 cup all-purpose flour
1 teaspoon baking powder
1/4 teaspoon nutmeg
1/2 teaspoon salt
2 1/2 tablespoons granulated sugar
1/3 cup fresh milk
2 eggs
Sliced freestone peaches

Dribble fresh lemon juice over the sliced peaches to keep them from turning brown. Soak the crushed leaves of fresh thyme in the lemon juice to add an exciting flavor.

Begin heating oil to 375 degrees. In a mixing bowl, combine the flour, baking powder, nutmeg, salt, and granulated sugar. Add eggs and milk gradually. Beat with egg beater (or whisk) until smooth. Dip fresh peaches into batter and drop into hot oil. Let fry about three minutes, turning once during that time, until golden. Drain, and sprinkle with powdered or pounded sugar. Serve hot. This will make about eighteen fritters.

1846 Fried Salt Pork

Old-time salt pork (fried) with cream gravy has a pull that does not lessen as the years go rolling by.

Salt pork
Fine cornmeal
Flour
Oil for frying

To make this treat, slice the pork thin. Take off the rind and slash one edge of the slices so that they will not curl as they fry. "Freshen" the pork a little by soaking it in ice-cold water or by parboiling it for a few minutes to remove the excess salt.

Dry the slices thoroughly in a cloth. Mix an equal quantity of fine cornmeal and flour and dip each slice in this. Fry in a hot frying pan until brown and crisp.

CREAM GRAVY
Pork fat
2 tablespoons flour
1/2 cup milk
1/2 cup cream

Blend well the pork fat with the flour. Add the milk and cream. Cook in a double-boiler, stirring all the time, until smooth and creamy and free from a single lump. Season with practically no salt but fairly highly with black pepper.

RECEIPTS FROM VARIOUS
Alabama Towns

Sweet Toncha

The true natives of Alabama were, of course, red men. In 1519 the history of Alabama's Indians first began to be recorded. The Spanish explorer Pineda spent around forty days in the Mobile area repairing his ships. He found a large Indian village on the bay and around the upper part of the Mobile River.

The Indians had numerous legends, similar to the myths of ancient Greece, that explained natural phenomena. Their favorite subjects were the creation, floods, and eclipses. There were many versions of the legends explaining the origins of corn. One was that it was the gift of an "Unknown Woman"; another said it was the gift of a child; another, that a black crow brought a single grain from a distant land and gave it to an orphan child.

Here is one favorite legend used to explain corn's origin:
The story goes that two Choctaw hunters were spending the night by a watch fire in the bed of the Alabama River. Every new moon the fish and game became very scarce, and on that particular night all they had to eat was the tough flesh of a black hawk.

As they mused upon their unfortunate condition, they thought of their hungry children and became very despondent, but they roasted the bird and started to eat it. Hardly had they commenced when they heard a noise resembling the cooing of a dove.

They jumped up and looked up and down the river's banks but could see nothing except the dark waters. They turned their faces in the direction opposite the moon and, to their dismay, discovered standing upon the summit of a grassy mound the form of a very beautiful woman.

They rushed to her side, and she told them she was very hungry. The hunters ran for their roasted hawk and placed the entire bird in her hands. She barely tasted the hawk but told the men that their kindness had saved her from starvation.

She promised that she would not forget them and that when she returned to the happy ground of her father, Hosh-tal-li, meaning Great Spirit of the Choctaws, they would be rewarded. She made one additional request of the men: when the next moon of midsummer should arrive, they must visit the spot where they had first seen her. Then a breeze swept across the river, and the strange woman disappeared.

These hunters went home to their families, keeping all they had seen and heard hidden in their hearts. Summer came, and they kept their promise to the beautiful woman and returned to the mounds on the banks of the Alabama River. They were amazed to find the ground there covered with a new plant whose leaves looked like the knives of the white man. That same summer, this strange plant yielded a delicious food that the Choctaws called Sweet Toncha, or Indian maize.

    4 or 5 ears fresh corn
    1 pint fairly heavy cream
    2 eggs
    2 tablespoons fresh butter
    Salt and pepper

Preheat the oven to 325 degrees. Grate the corn from the cob. Do not cut. Beat the eggs; add them to the corn; add the cream, melted butter, salt, and pepper. Mix well. Bake in a moderate oven for about thirty minutes. Do not let the corn get hot enough to boil or the eggs and cream will separate. This may sound like an ordinary pudding, but the grating of the corn makes a difference.

Summertime Fresh Corn Fritters

Some folks say preachers won't steal,
But I caught three in my cornfield.
One had a bushel, one had a peck,
One had a roastin' ear hung 'round his neck.

According to a note written in the margins of this receipt, it came from Beaver Creek, Alabama, and was handed down from Martha Silas Lovejoy, whose husband fought and died at Fort Mims in 1813. She herself was scalped by the Indians in 1817.

2 1/2 cups fresh corn pulp
2 egg yolks, well beaten
1 cup fresh milk (less if corn is loose)
1 1/4 cups flour
1 teaspoon baking powder
Salt and pepper to taste
2 egg whites, stiffly beaten
Hot fat

Cut the corn from the cob and scrape the cob well with the back of a knife to get all the milk from the ear. Mix the flour, baking powder, and seasoning; add this mixture to the corn and mix. Beat the egg yolks and add them to the corn mixture. Then add the milk. Beat the egg whites stiff and fold them in. Drop by spoonfuls into the hot fat (shallow or deep fry). Fry until golden brown.

Real Alabama Pie Crust

This crust has been made in the South for more than one hundred years. It never fails . . . for a Southerner, that is.

1/8 cup boiling water
1/4 cup pure hog lard
2/3 cup self-rising flour
1 tablespoon sugar

Pour the boiling water over the lard. Beat until the lard melts. Sift in the flour. Roll out the dough and line the pie plate. If you like, you can brush the crust with sugar and prick the top with the tines of a fork.

Old-Timey Steamed Okra

A man called King Pharr was born in Lower Peach Tree, Alabama, and was known all over the United States as the "Okra King." His canned okra had a superior quality that has never been duplicated.

He was the son of John W. and Alabama King Pharr. The King family played an important role in the founding of Judson College in Marion, Alabama, in the early 1800s.

To eat okra as it was meant to be eaten, pick very young okra pods and leave the stems on. Very carefully place the pods over boiling water in a double boiler. Cover and steam for about fifteen minutes. Serve with hot melted butter. Hold the okra by the stem, dip it in the hot butter, carry it to your mouth, and nature will do the rest.

Marsh Hens

This receipt comes from Huntsville, Alabama, and was found in an account book dated 1837. The book bears the name of Jedediah Lovette. On June 19, 1837, his account was credited seventy cents for one day's work chopping wood. For hoeing corn, he was credited with eighty-three cents for one day's work. Hoeing corn was apparently harder than chopping wood.

Huntsville, the home of this receipt, was the scene of great commotion on the night of November 12, 1833, remembered as the night stars fell on Alabama. There was temporarily a great revival among the Christians who interpreted the falling stars as a sign of approaching doom.

At five o'clock on Wednesday morning, it was cool, clear, and extremely beautiful. The stars shone with uncommon brilliancy. Thousands of luminous meteors were shooting across the firmament in every direction. Their course was from the center of the concave toward the horizon. Then they seemed to explode. It appeared as if the stars were really "falling." The scene was beautiful and magnificent. The meteors succeeded each other in quick succession until early dawn, producing a scene of true nocturnal grandeur.

People still say that the starfish found on the beaches today are those very stars that fell into the sea and were transformed, just as the sea, in myths and legends, has changed many things into living creatures throughout time. Conjure women say this branded Alabama as a strange land and forever set her people apart by a horoscope of turmoil and enchantment.

Marsh hens are a delectable game bird, about the size of a broiling chicken. Found along the marshes and the coast and hunted in the fall, these birds are skinned instead of picked.

Cut their legs off at the first joint where the feathers begin. Carefully pull the skin back to the body. Split the skin between the legs, cutting just through the outside skin. Peel all the skin off, cutting off the wing joints and head. Split the bird down the back and clean it, saving the giblets. Wash it well and put it in the icebox. If you don't have an icebox, place it in the coolest place in the spring house.

Since the flavor of marsh hens is so delicate, never soak them in salt water. When you are ready to cook the birds, dry them off and dip them in red wine, then in a mixture of flour, salt, and pepper. Fry them to a golden brown.

Buttermilk Biscuits

Oh, when I die bury me deep,
With a jug of 'lasses at my feet,
Two big biscuits in my han',
And I'll sop my way to the Promised Land.

This receipt came from Tuscaloosa, Alabama, the town that was named for the Indian chief Tuscaloosa. It was in the time of DeSoto (1540) that Chief Tuscaloosa became angry at the brutality and arrogance of the white invaders. Legend has it that the tall Indian spread his arms and intoned, "Cursed by the white man with his evil ways who kills my people. The waters of our land will avenge the death of our warriors. The waters will consume our enemies. As long as the [Black Warrior] river flows, it will take the white man as a sacrifice."

People believe that drownings in the Black Warrior are a part of Tuscaloosa's curse. There has never been a year since he voiced the curse without a number of drownings. Due to the river's dark waters, locating bodies is difficult, and there is an old superstition that if a white shirt belonging to a drowned person is thrown into the river near where the drowning occurred, the shirt will float directly over the body.

Somewhere in Clarke County, Alabama, DeSoto was invited to visit Chief Tuscaloosa and to find "friendship and peace" wherever he chose to pass through the territory controlled by the chief. Instead, he met death and disaster. The great battle was at Mauvilla (a place name for which the spelling has since changed many times) on October 18, 1540. The exact spot is unknown. It is believed that Tuscaloosa perished and that DeSoto did not return to Pensacola, Florida, to meet his waiting ship but instead turned northwest and died of yellow fever. He was buried in the Mississippi River.

> 2 cups all-purpose flour
> 1 teaspoon salt
> 1/2 teaspoon soda
> 1 teaspoon baking powder
> 3 tablespoons butter or pure lard
> 3/4 to 1 cup buttermilk

Preheat the oven to 400 degrees. Combine the flour, soda, salt, and baking powder. Cut in the shortening and mix until the ingredients resemble coarse meal. Stir in just enough buttermilk to make a soft dough. Turn the dough on a floured surface and roll to about one-half-inch thickness. Cut with a small glass or napkin ring. Bake in a fairly hot oven for fifteen minutes. This will make about sixteen biscuits.

To remove mildew, soak the stained material in sour buttermilk. Then spread it in the hot sun.

Selma Bourbon Sweet Potatoes

This receipt came from Selma, Alabama, where the story is still told of the young Presbyterian minister killed in the Battle of Selma. As friends bore the body of the young minister into the manse on a beautiful April day, they walked under the arched branches of a Lady Banksia rose. When they passed beneath the climbing rose, it shed its yellow petals like gentle tears upon the body of the Reverend Arthur M. small in a tearful blessing.

That same Lady Banksia rose is said still to bloom each spring at the Presbyterian Church in Selma as a reminder of the day that Selma wept.

A note at the bottom of this receipt says:

> You might get by ol' man "need more,"
> But you sho can't get by ol' "have to have."

4 pounds sweet potatoes
1/2 cup pure butter
1/4 cup fine bourbon
1/3 cup fresh orange juice
1/4 cup slightly browned sugar
1 teaspoon salt
1/2 teaspoon cinnamon and nutmeg, mixed
1/3 chopped pecans

Preheat the oven to 350 degrees. Cook and mash the sweet potatoes. Add the butter, bourbon, orange juice, salt, and spices. Beat well. Put the mixture into a buttered pan and sprinkle with the pecans. Bake for about forty-five minutes.

The story goes that a Mrs. Hobbos of Selma was a very religious woman who believed that dancing was a sin. During the Civil War she quilted diamonds and watches into her wide petticoat to keep them from the plundering Yankee soldiers. She hid bags of silver and her husband's jewelry behind the weatherboarding on her back porch. When she learned that dancing was a necessary part of Yankees' lives, she referred the men to Mobile to be measured for tuxedos. She told them, "If you have to go to hell, I want you to go looking like gentlemen."

Marinated Rattlesnake

This receipt was written in a ledger that came from Limestone, Alabama, a community along the banks of the Little River. It no longer exists under that name. The Little River was infested with snakes.

Corrie, the Faulk housekeeper, said of this receipt, "A body has got to be bad off for somethin' to eat." Truman's comment was that it was "a mouthful."

Remove the head and skin from the rattlesnake (hang him in the fork of a tree to skin him). Look carefully to see if he has bitten himself. They can. Do not eat him if he has.

Clean and cut the meat into two-inch pieces and marinate them in the juice of oranges and lemons with a teaspoon of peppercorns and a dash of nutmeg.

If you have gotten this far, drain the snake meat and wipe it dry. Sprinkle it with salt and fresh pepper and dip the pieces in beaten egg, then roll them in fine bread crumbs. Slowly cook the snake meat in hot butter until each piece is golden brown.

Always keep rattlesnake skin handy to bind around the waist for rheumatism.

The Piney Woods Country

The Piney Woods country is deep in Alabama's Tombigbee swamp. There you will find frightened deer bounding across the highway, and wild turkeys, bears, ducks, and all manner of small game flourishing beside alligator-infested sloughs. Here, too, are rich limestone valleys, rolling hills, and sandy levels where the odor of resinous pine scents the air and the tall trees moan with the wind. Late in the afternoon you can see the purple shadows and smoke hanging above the tree tops, announcing the cheery news of supper cooking or the still making a run.

This area produced several of the receipts that Sook collected over the years, among them receipts for venison roast, a post-hunt breakfast, ham and red-eye gravy, and baked fresh tomatoes.

Escambia Creek Venison Roast

1 venison roast (5–6 pounds)
Sherry
1 fresh onion
1/4 teaspoon ginger
Salt to taste
1 large bay leaf
2 cloves fresh garlic
3 slices thick bacon
1 tablespoon fresh pepper
1/4 cup fresh parsley

Place the roast in a large pan and pour in enough water and sherry to cover it. Add the onion, pepper, garlic, and bay leaf. Let the roast stand, covered, in the refrigerator for two to three days.

Preheat the oven to 325 degrees. When you are ready to cook the roast, sear it on all sides. Salt all sides. In a heavy iron pot with one-and-a-half cups of the marinade, cook the roast until tender.

Add the ginger to the gravy only. Fry the bacon and crumble it into the parsley. Sprinkle this mixture on top of the roast just before serving.

After-the-Hunt Breakfast

1/2 cup pure butter
1/2 cup onions, finely chopped
1/2 teaspoon salt
3 tablespoons flour
1 cup milk
6 hard-boiled eggs, finely diced
2 cups cooked ham, diced
1/2 cup fresh mushrooms, precooked and sliced
Pinch white pepper
1 cup coffee cream

Sauté the onions in butter until they are transparent. Add the salt, pepper, and flour. Cook over a low heat, stirring all the while. Slowly add the cream and milk. Cook until the mixture thickens. Remove from the heat and add the ham, eggs, and mushrooms. Stir and sprinkle lightly with white pepper. Serve on hot toast or with hot grits.

Clean fingertips and nails by digging into a grapefruit hull leftover from breakfast.

Ham and Red-Eye Gravy

Cut a center slice of a ham about three-quarters of an inch thick in two pieces and brown on both sides in a hot iron skillet. Make slashes all around the edges of the ham's fat to keep the ham from buckling up while it cooks. After the ham is well browned on both sides and is done, turn the heat up, and when it is smoking (be careful not to burn it), turn the heat off and pour one-half cup of cold coffee over the ham along with about one-half cup of cold water. This will turn the gravy red. Serve with the ham and grits.

Piney Woods Baked Fresh Tomatoes

6 fresh tomatoes
2 teaspoons salt
1 tablespoon butter
1 cup fresh milk
4 slices bacon
2 tablespoons flour
Pepper to taste
1/2 cup fresh mushrooms
Generous amount of parsley for topping

Preheat the oven to 325 degrees. Cut the tomatoes in halves without peeling them and place them in a baking dish with the cut side up, making cups of the tomatoes. Sprinkle with the salt and pepper. Cut the bacon into pieces and put one piece on each tomato half. Bake for thirty minutes. Put the cooked tomatoes on a platter.

Make a brown sauce as follows: Melt the butter, add the flour, and allow the mixture to brown. Mash up one of the cooked tomatoes in the sauce, using any juice or brown part that accumulated in the cooking. Add the mushrooms, cooking lightly, pour the sauce over the tomatoes, and serve. Sprinkle the tomatoes and sauce with a generous amount of fresh parsley.

Cornmeal Dumplings

This receipt comes from Montgomery, Alabama, the Cradle of the Confederacy. In the heart of Montgomery, an artesian well flows where the present Court Square fountain is located.

Before the white man came, Indians drank the crystal waters form this well and praised their ancestral God for its blessings. The Indian legend promised prosperity and power to people living near the spring for as long as the well flowed.

As Montgomery grew, some citizens decided that something should be done to beautify the artesian well beyond the plain iron fence that surrounded it. They felt that a touch of elegance was needed. In 1880 the city council purchased a bronze fountain, a work of Frederick McMonnies that had been shown at the Atlanta Exposition. The fountain was a life-sized figure of Hebe, the goddess of youth and spring, the daughter of Zeus and Hera and the wife of Hercules. Hebe topped the fountain and graceful nymphs posed around the lower tiers. It was erected at the artesian base on Court Square and dedicated on the seventeenth of October, 1885.

Some people in Montgomery were not too happy over Hebe. Some thought her a little naughty, but the main problems, initially, were water pumps that burned out, a lack of sufficient water power, and the color of the protective paint over the bronze. Matters worsened when the nymphs began falling from their perches, and the final blow came when Hebe herself toppled!

But good news ultimately prevailed. Hebe is back, recast one hundred pounds lighter and more youthful in appearance. The water now spews gracefully, and the lights make visiting the fountain feel almost like sliding into sunshine.

Tied as it is to Indian legend about the famed well, Montgomery has grown strong and prospered.

On a pedestrian island a few feet from Hebe is a plain stand with a heavy glass cover. Under the cover is a big family Bible, placed there in 1945 by Ben Davis, owner of a Montgomery printing company. Thousands of people passing through the downtown area pause to read a few verses of scripture.

During his lifetime, Mr. Davis chose different passages from the Bible to feature at the display. The Psalms and the Gospels were his favorites. Since his death, the Davis family has continued the tradition.

1 cup freshly ground cornmeal
1 1/2 cups boiling water
1 tablespoon sugar
1/2 teaspoon salt
1 egg

Gradually add the cornmeal to the boiling water, stir vigorously, and cook until a thick mush is formed. Add the sugar and salt and cool. Add the egg and beat well. Drop the batter by tablespoonfuls on a floured board, roll into small balls, and dredge with flour. Drop into boiling liquid and cook slowly for about fifteen minutes. Dumplings can be made in broth from fresh collard or turnip greens or chicken or ham broth.

In the South, we call this dish Pot Liquor.

Some folks would call this dish Pot Likker.

Fried Apples

This receipt, more than one hundred years old, comes from Brewton, Alabama.

Pollard, Alabama, was the county seat for Escambia County, but the town of Brewton felt that it should be the county seat. When the courthouse in Pollard burned in 1880, Brewton thought it was time to move the seat of government to their town. Pollard didn't see it that way at all and a real squabble ensued.

It was decided that an election would settle the issue, but it turned out that Pollard had about 130 more votes than there were registered voters. Brewton demanded a recount.

After much legal maneuvering, another election gave the courthouse to Brewton. Pollard, however, refused to relinquish the country records or the title of county seat. The fighting and bickering became so intense that a Brewton man likened it to an ordinary cat fight. The idea appealed to the people of Pollard. They issued a statement to Brewton, "If it's a cat fight you want, we will do our share."

Shortly afterward, a boxcar arrived at the depot in Brewton with a strange cargo. When the doors of the boxcar were opened, hundreds of cats and kittens jumped out. Brewton was completely overrun with cats. They finally got the courthouse and the records and the title of county seat, but folks in Brewton also still have more cats than any other town in Alabama.

> 6 fresh apples
> 2 tablespoons butter
> 2 tablespoons sugar
> 2 tablespoons molasses
> 1 tablespoon water

Cut the apples into eighths. Peel just one strip of skin from each piece. Melt the butter in a skillet. Add the molasses, water, and sugar. Mix well. Add the apple slices and cook, covered, until they are tender. Remove the cover and cook until all the juice is boiled away and the apples are brown.

Chicken Jefferson

This receipt comes from Birmingham, Alabama, home of Charles Linn, a prominent pioneer of that city. Linn issued invitations to a Calico Ball to be held on the night of December 31, 1873. The ball was to celebrate that passing of the cholera and the opening of the National Bank of Birmingham, of which he was president. The scene of the ball was the second floor of the bank building.

About five hundred written invitations were issues, and around 9:00 P.M. on the last night of 1873 the guests assembled to dance the old year out and the new in. A band from Montgomery, led by a Mr. DeJarnette, came to Birmingham to play especially for the event. Mr. and Mrs. Linn took the lead in the grand march, bringing all the dancers to the floor. The hosts and their guests danced the Virginia reel, the cotillion, lancers, a Spanish dance, and the round dance.

The ladies wore calico evening gowns, some with trains of various colors and trimmings, some donning shepherd checks and others black dresses trimmed with ermine. The gallant Southern gentlemen wore full-dress suits of calico. Mr. Linn's dark brown-and-tan calico suit attracted quite a bit of attention with its huge buttons.

Sandwiches and coffee were served on the first floor, after which the guests again assembled in the ballroom for the midnight hour. On the stroke of twelve, all stopped dancing and stood quietly to observe the passing of 1873 and the dawn of 1874, marked by the lifting of a screen revealing the figures of 1873, which was then superceded by the dropping of a second screen, emblazoned with 1874, over the first. The ball continued until 2:30 A.M.

The social life represented by this ball also produced some of the South's finest foods. Chicken Jefferson is one of those fine dishes. Truman remembered this receipt fondly, saying, "After many Sunday dinners and idle conversation, we could at last sit on the doorstep in the moonlight, utterly content—nice memories."

8 chicken breasts
1/2 cup butter
3 tablespoons sherry
1/2 pound fresh mushrooms
3 tablespoons flour
2 cups chicken broth
1 tablespoon thick tomato paste
1 fresh bay leaf
3 tablespoons chopped fresh chives
1/2 teaspoon salt
1/4 teaspoon fresh pepper
1 cup fresh shrimp, cooked
1 sprig fresh mint

Preheat the oven to 300 degrees. Sauté the chicken breasts in the butter until they are golden brown. Spoon on the sherry. Put the chicken in a baking dish and cover. Bake for about thirty minutes.

In a skillet, sauté the mushrooms in butter and blend in the flour. Add the chicken broth, tomato paste, and seasonings and simmer until the mixture thickens. Add the cooked seafood and simmer until thoroughly heated. Serve the sauce over the chicken.

Enterprise Peanut Brittle

This receipt comes from Enterprise, Alabama, located in Coffee County, deep in the heart of peanut country. Enterprise has the world's only monument erected to honor a pest. People seeing it for the first time are surprised by the lady, draped in a classic Grecian robe, holding aloft a large copper-plated boll weevil.

The story goes that the Mexican boll weevil invaded Coffee County in 1915 and completely destroyed the cotton crops. The next year the same thing happened. In pure desperation, farms turned from cotton to corn, hay, sugar cane, potatoes, and peanuts. Millions of bushels of peanuts were produced.

In gratitude for this new agricultural prosperity, the city decided to erect a monument to the boll weevil. The monument was unveiled on December 11, 1919. The inscription on its base reads, "In Profound Appreciation of the Boll Weevil and What It Has Done as the Herald of Prosperity. This Monument Was Erected by the Citizens of Enterprise, Coffee County, Alabama."

1 cup sugar
1/2 cup white Karo syrup
1/4 cup hot water
1 teaspoon butter
2 cups raw peanuts
1 teaspoon soda
1 teaspoon pure vanilla

Bring the syrup, sugar, and water to a boil. Add the butter and peanuts. Boil and stir constantly until the peanuts start to pop and the syrup starts to brown. Remove from the heat and add vanilla and soda. Remove from the heat and add vanilla and soda. Work very fast. Pour on a greased marble slab, smooth out, and let cool. Break into chunks and serve or store.

Coastal Specialties

The Alabama coast is seafood country. From where the slender piers edge out into Mobile Bay at Bon Secour, Point Clear, Daphne, and Battles Wharf come crab gumbo, broiled flounder, oyster stew, shrimp jambalaya, and red snapper. That strange phenomenon, the "Jubilee," when fish, shrimp, and crab rush from the water and onto the shore to be gathered up in buckets and dishpans and taken home to be eaten, occurs each year.

Knowing your fish is very easy when you follow these simple guidelines: 1) The flesh should be firm and spring back when it is pressed with the fingers. 2) The scales should be firmly attached and sparkle like diamonds. 3) The eyes should be well rounded, not sunken. 4) The gills should be a brilliant red. 5) The fish should have an odor that is light, mild, fresh. Smell the gills to be sure that they have a fresh odor.

Baked Stuffed Snapper

1 pound fresh shrimp, peeled and deveined
1 large onion, chopped
2 cloves fresh garlic, minced
1 tablespoon butter, melted
1/4 cup water
6 slices bread
1 small green pepper, finely chopped
2 tablespoons fresh parsley, chopped

1 tablespoon celery, chopped
1 pint fresh oysters, drained and chopped
3/4 teaspoon salt
1/4 teaspoon pepper
1 bay leaf
1/2 teaspoon thyme
8 red snapper fillets (approximately 4 pounds)
Creole Sauce

Preheat the oven to 350 degrees. Sauté the shrimp, onion, and garlic in shortening in a large iron skillet for about fifteen minutes over medium heat. Sprinkle water over the bread, mash, and add the shrimp mixture. Add all the other ingredients and simmer for ten minutes. Place four large fillets on the broiler pan; evenly spoon one-quarter of the mixture on each fillet. Top with the remaining fillets and fasten with wooden toothpicks. Pour the creole sauce over the fish and bake for thirty minutes or until the fillets flake easily when tested with the tines of a fork.

Transfer the stuffed fillets to a large platter and serve.

CREOLE SAUCE
2 large onions, finely chopped
2 cloves garlic, minced
1 green pepper, finely chopped
2 tablespoons fresh parsley, chopped
2 bay leaves
1 pinch dried thyme
1 tablespoon melted shortening
1 tablespoon all-purpose flour
1 16-ounch can tomatoes, undrained and chopped

Sauté the first six ingredients in the shortening in a large skillet for about fifteen minutes over low heat. Add the flour, and cook for one minute, stirring constantly. Stir in the tomatoes and simmer for ten minutes. Pour over the snapper before baking it.

Redfish Fillets with Crabmeat Sauce

6 or 7 redfish fillets
1 pound fresh crabmeat
1/2 pound fresh butter
1/2 cup fresh shallots, chopped fine
1 clove fresh garlic, chopped fine
1 1/2 teaspoons fresh parsley, chopped fine
1/8 teaspoon cayenne pepper
1/4 teaspoon paprika
1/2 cup breadcrumbs
Lettuce leaves for each fish fillet
1 1/2 cups heavy cream
2 tablespoons all-purpose flour
1 egg, well beaten
Salt and white pepper to taste
1/2 cup white wine

Preheat the oven to 350 degrees and place the fillets, skin side down, in a large greased baking pan and set aside. Melt one tablespoon of butter in a saucepan, add the shallots, half of the crabmeat, the garlic, parsley, paprika, and cayenne pepper. Cook until the shallots are clear in color. Add the breadcrumbs. Remove from the heat and let cool. Spread the crabmeat mixture on the fillets. Pour boiling water over the lettuce leaves to wilt them. Roll the fillets and wrap them in the wilted lettuce leaves. Return the fillets to the pan and bake for forty-five minutes.

Melt the remaining butter in a pan, add the flour, and make a roux. Stir while cooking for about five minutes. Gradually add heavy cream, slowly stirring to keep the mixture smooth. Add the egg, white pepper, and salt, stirring constantly. Add the remaining crabmeat and the wine. Cook for only three minutes. Remove from the heat. Take the stuff rolls of fish from the oven and place them on a heated platter. Pour the crabmeat sauce over them.

This dish serves around eight people.

(Redfish are sometimes called channel bass or drum.)

Sweet Potato Pie

This receipt is from Old Manistee, Alabama, and had the name Aunt Pallie written in its margins.

> 4 medium sweet potatoes, quartered
> 4 tablespoons butter, softened
> 3/4 cup dark brown sugar
> 3 eggs, slightly beaten
> 1/3 cup light corn syrup
> 1/3 cup milk (cream not removed)
> 2 teaspoons fresh lemon peel, finely grated
> 1 teaspoon vanilla extract
> 1/4 teaspoon ground fresh nutmeg
> 1/2 teaspoon salt

Have ready one eight-inch pie crust shell. Drop the quartered sweet potatoes into enough boiling water to immerse them. Boil them briskly, uncovered, until they are tender when pierced with a fork. Rub the sweet potatoes through a fine sieve with the back of a spoon.

Preheat the oven to 300 degrees. In a deep bowl, cream the butter and brown sugar together by beating and mashing them against the sides of the bowl with the back of a wooden spoon until they are light and fluffy. Beat in the mashed potatoes, add the eggs, one at a time, beating well after each one. Add the light corn syrup, milk, lemon peel, vanilla, grated nutmeg, and salt and continue to beat until the filling is smooth.

Pour the mixture into the pie shell. First bake for fifteen minutes in the middle of the oven set at 300 degrees and then raise the oven temperature to 325 degrees and bake for an additional thirty-five minutes.

Women in the South had to fight for survival during and after the Civil War. Sugar became scarce, so sorghum became the standard sweetener. The women learned to make a substitute for ordinary baking soda from the ashes of corn cobs. These ashes were placed in a jar and covered with water to stand until clear. By using one part ashes and two parts sour milk, various sweet items could be made.

French Strawberry Preserves

This receipt came from White Bluff, Alabama (now Demopolis). The French arrived in Alabama in 1818, following Napoleon's final defeat at Waterloo in 1815, in fear for their lives. Nearly forty leading Bonapartists had been ordered to leave Paris within three days. Others were exiled. In either case, some fled to America and eventually settled in Alabama.

Henry Clay (1777–1852), the statesman, was instrumental in getting Congress to grant to the French 92,160 acres of public land along the Tombigbee River. The French were to pay two dollars per acre over a period of fourteen years.

They planted olives and vines, but their colony was a failure from the start. Gradually they moved to Mobile or New Orleans; some even returned to France. The French were the first to introduce black slavery into Alabama, and the French ladies brought with them the custom of going to a slaughterhouse to swallow a glass of blood for medicinal purposes.

Although an 1870 cookbook published in Paris during the siege of that city gave recipes for preparing rats and dogs, most French food more than deserves its reputation for culinary greatness. These preserves certainly do. Truman's comment: "Christ! This makes my mouth water. Make me some!"

Wash and cap large, firm, ripe berries, washing quickly so as not to watersoak them. For every pound of berries, allow three-quarters of a pound of sugar.

Sprinkle the sugar over the berries and let them stand for several hours until a syrup is formed. Place the sugared berries over a fire, bring them to a boil, and let them continue to boil gently for one minute. Remove them from the fire and set them in a cool place to stand overnight. The following day again bring the berries to a boil and allow them to boil for two minutes, then again stand overnight. On the third day, repeat the process, this time allowing the boiling to go on for three minutes. Pour the fruit into sterilized jars and seal with paraffin immediately.

Sweetin' Biscuits

This receipt comes from the Holly family of Prairie Bluff (Prairie Blue). They came to Alabama from England.

Prairie Bluff was a river landing on the high bluff on the north bank of the Alabama River. It was listed on the state map of 1822 as "Prairie Blue," but on all subsequent maps it is called Prairie Bluff. A large cotton slide was erected from the top of the bluff to the wharf below. Engravings show black men loading the cotton at night under the light of torches.

On October 28, 1841, the steamboat *Jewess* struck a snag and sank. The same fate had befallen another steamer, the *Pittsburg,* there in May 1828. The landing reached its peak around 1861, but after the Civil War the railroads captured the river trade and the town died.

It was either in Prairie Bluff or Claiborne (they are very near each other) that a Union soldier rode a bale of cotton to his death. Both these towns are situated on the highest bluffs along the banks of the Alabama River, and the drop to the landings below is hundreds of feet. A track, or tramway, was laid on which a car was lowered and hauled by means of a rope, which was secured around a vertical windlass with a horse or an ox moving in a circle.

This car was used to transport freight. Between car tracks, a slide for the bales of cotton being shipped to Mobile made loading the boats easier. It was probably a quarter of a mile down the slide. When you stood at the top of the bluff and looked down, the steamboats looked like toys.

In the winter of 1865, Claiborne and Prairie Bluff were headquarters for a part of Sherman's army, and the area was filled with Yankee soldiers. The warehouses for the cotton had numerous sheds erected around them to house additional cotton, and these sheds became a campground for the Yankees. That meant that they were always around when a steamboat arrived.

The boats always whistled before they reached the landing. The warehouse clerk notified the boat as to the number of bales to be loaded for Mobile. Gangplanks were thrown out, and some seven or eight bales of cotton were rolled off the boat and piled up as a bulwark to stop the bales that were meant to be sent down the slide.

Some of the black men were sent to the warehouse to start the cotton down the slide. The first bales moved very slowly over the wooden slide, but the more they sent down, the faster each one went, until they reached a speed that was almost frightening. It was a custom for some of the black hands to take a ride on the first bales by lying down and holding the bagging on the side of the bale.

One day, the story goes, the Yankee soldiers were at the landing, drinking, when the cotton was rolled out to be placed on the slide. As was the custom, three or four of the dock hands straddled the cotton to enjoy the slow but hazardous ride to the boat. One of the drunken Yankee soldiers took a notion to ride down the slide on a bale of cotton himself. All the other soldiers tried to discourage him, but he persisted in his foolishness and laid himself out full length upon a bale as he had seen the black men do.

By this time the slide had become very slick, and the deck hands tried to step in where the soldier's friends had failed and prevent the soldier from taking the ride. But the bale he had chosen started down with the Yankee still on it.

The bale started slowly at first but gained speed at an alarming rate. When it struck the bales at the landing, those watching spotted a speck of blue shooting across the bow of the boat. There was a splash in the river and one less soldier in Sherman's army.

1 whole egg, plus one extra yolk
2 cups all-purpose flour, well-sifted
1/2 cup milk
1/2 teaspoon salt
2 teaspoons baking powder
1/4 cup powdered sugar
6 tablespoons unsalted butter
1/4 cup raisins
1/4 cup chopped walnuts

Scones, as they are called today, are becoming very popular, but all my life I have enjoyed these sweetened biscuits. Probably the only difference between the ones I grew up with and the ones currently being cooked is that we dropped ours by a teaspoon onto a buttered pan and the modern ones are usually rolled out. The secret to making scones is to mix them as quickly as possible with as little handling as possible. The oven should be preheated to 450 degrees.

Beat the egg and the extra yolk just enough to mix them. Add the milk and set the mixture aside. Sift together the flour, baking powder, sugar, and salt. Add the butter and cut it into the mixture until it resembles coarse meal (lumps of butter should be about the size of a dried pea). Stir in the raisins and the walnuts. Add the egg mixture all at once, and stir with a fork as quickly as possible until all the dry ingredients are barely moist.

Spoon out a rounded tablespoon of the batter and drop it on the buttered pan or baking sheet. Bake for around fifteen minutes until the scones are an uneven brown. Serve at once with homemade preserves.

Lafayette's Visit to Claiborne, Alabama

Claiborne is in Monroe County on the bluff of the Alabama River between Montgomery and Mobile. Its elevation of two hundred feet above the water of the river gives it an appearance of romance. The view from the west and the northwest is quite picturesque.

Claiborne is watered by innumerable clear springs that issue from the bluff and throw themselves headlong into the river below, forming beautiful cascades. Every few years, however, the river rises like a monster from its bed and rushes over the banks to vex and sweeten the land it has made. The earth is sweet-smelling and dark brown, built over centuries as the by-product of the river's natural task of cleansing itself.

The French general Marquis de Lafayette, famous for his aid to the American colonists in their fight for freedom, visited Claiborne on April 5, 1825. A letter of invitation had been written by James Dellet, a congressman from the Whig Party. It read:

> General Lafayette:
> Sir:
>
> The citizens of the county of Monroe and town of Claiborne; having participated in common with the American people, in the unfeigned gladness of heart imparted by the certain information of your arrival in the United States, desire me to say to you that it will afford them a gratification which they anticipate with the most grateful feelings, if you can make it convenient to touch at Claiborne on your passage from

Montgomery to Mobile and afford them the pleasure of your company for such time as you can spare under the arrangements of your western tour.

I am with very great respect,

Your obt. James Dellet
Chairman of the Committee of Claiborne
21st March, 1825

General Lafayette and his entourage, with his son, George Washington Lafayette, traveling by boat on the Alabama River from Montgomery to Mobile, spent the afternoon and evening in the town as a result of this invitation.

A reception at the Dellet home was given, complete with refreshments and dinner. The bill of fare was headed by six hams, followed by eight roast turkeys, six roast suckling pigs, twenty-four hens, twelve ducks, and six dishes of roast beef, with all the appropriate trimmings and vegetables. Later in the Town Hall oratory and entertainment were provided.

Lavasseur, secretary to the general, records in his journal, *The Tour of America,* that Lafayette and members of his party were amazed at the elegance of the Dellet home, with its dark marble fireplaces, great mirrors, hand-painted china, and fine silver. They were especially impressed by the great secretary that graced the Dellet hallway. This piece of furniture had been specially shipped from England.

Claiborne takes its name from old Fort Claiborne, built during General Andrew Jackson's war against the Creek Indians, whose leader was William Weatherford, also known as Red Eagle.

In its early days, Claiborne was a very important river trading point. A boat landing and dock were built on the river bank, two hundred feet below the town. Steamboats traveling from New Orleans and Mobile brought merchandise and equipment into the town's warehouse and picked up bales of cotton.

Under the warehouse a big rope was connected to a pulley and tied to a cart on a track. The pulley was trundled by a mule and pulled the cart loaded with cotton or freight to and from the landing below. A flight of 365 (for the days in the year) wooden steps was built from the landing up to the town. The track is almost gone, but its remains can still be seen and some of the steps are still there.

Today, a traveler would see only a ghost of what once was a thriving and important Southern town. It had a population of more than eight thousand, with busy streets, important buildings, and fine pretentious homes. Once it was the state's second largest city, failing by only one vote to become the capital of Alabama.

Typical
Sunday Dinner Receipts

Roast Chicken According to Scriptural Precepts

According to a preacher who traveled the back roads of the South, there were Scriptural precepts for the carving of a roasted chicken.

It was the custom for families to invite the traveling preacher for Sunday dinner. The head of the house received the head of the chicken. His wife, closest to him, received the neck, which is naturally closest to the chicken's head. The chicken wings, symbolic of flighty thoughts, belonged to the daughters of the family. The family's sons claimed rights to those mainstays of the chicken's anatomy, the drumsticks, which represented the future support of the household. Having ascribed the sanctioned portions to the various members of the family, the preacher was then able to eat heartily himself. The family dined wisely, if not well.

> 6- to 7-pound roasting chicken
> 1 1/2 cups fresh butter
> 2 small onions, finely chopped
> 2 fresh carrots, finely chopped
> 2 stalks celery, finely chopped
> Salt
> Freshly ground black pepper

Preheat the oven to 325 degrees. Put a six- or seven-pound roasting chicken, trussed, in a large baking pan with one-and-a-half cups fresh butter and two small onions, two fresh carrots, and two stalks of celery, all finely chopped. Sprinkle the chicken with salt and fresh ground black pepper and roast, basting frequently, for about two-and-a-half to three hours or until the juice that runs from the second joint, when pricked with the tines of a fork, has no tinge of pink. About ten minutes before the chicken is done, raise the oven heat to about 450 degrees to brown the bird.

During the days of the colonists, a wooden salt bowl was an essential part of the tableware. It was always placed near the center of the table and served as a dividing line distinguishing guests and those of high rank from the family.

Original Waldorf Salad

This receipt came from a plantation record book and is believed to be the same one that was served in 1893 at the original Fifth Avenue Waldorf Hotel in New York.

> 2 1/2 cups apple, diced with peels left on
> 1 1/2 cups celery strips, about 1/2 inch long
> 3/4 cup pecans, chopped
> 1 teaspoon lemon juice
> 1/2 cup mayonnaise
> Lettuce leaves

Blend all the ingredients except the lettuce. Serve on crisp lettuce leaves. Be sure to dribble lemon juice over the apples to keep them from browning.

Crackling Bread

Cracklings are the pieces of meat remaining after the lard has been rendered from fresh-killed pork.

> 1 1/2 cups cracklings, crushed
> 1 1/2 cups cornmeal
> 3/4 cup plain flour

1/2 teaspoon soda
1/4 teaspoon salt
1 cup sour milk

Preheat the oven to 400 degrees. Sift and mix together the dry ingredients. Add the milk and stir in the cracklings. Pat the mixture out in the palm of your hand to make small oblong cakes. Bake in a well-greased baking pan for about thirty minutes.

Carpetbaggers' Steak

The story goes that steak was fixed this way to fool Yankees. Many of them hated oysters and were very disappointed to find little steak and a lot of oysters in the dish. The general sentiment about Yankees was that they should have been hung when they were young enough that a potato vine would have done the job.

Get a sirloin steak about two-and-a-half to three inches thick. Be sure it is tender with plenty of marbling. Insert a sharp knife in the center on one side and slice horizontally to within one or two inches of the edge of the steak to make a pocket.

Stuff the pocket with eighteen to twenty-five raw oysters. Season with salt and pepper. Sew the edge of the opening together.

Broil the steak for about fifteen minutes on each side. Lower the flame and cook until the meat reaches the desired doneness. Serve with the pan drippings.

Dixie-Fried Chicken

1 frying chicken, 2 to 2 1/2 pounds
1 1/2 cups plain flour
1/2 teaspoon salt
1/2 teaspoon fresh ground black pepper
1/4 teaspoon ground ginger
1/3 cup pure butter
2/3 cup pure lard

Cut the chicken up into parts. Rinse and pat the pieces of the chicken dry. Put the dry ingredients in a brown paper bag and shake the chicken for a few minutes. When the fat is smoking hot, lay in the chicken without crowding the pieces. Cover the pan and cook until the under side is good and brown. Remove the cover, turn the pieces, and fry until the other side is a deep brown. Reduce the heat and let the chicken fry slowly until fork tender.

Green Corn Spoon Bread

2 cups fresh milk

1/3 cup cornmeal

3 ears corn, cut very fine

2 eggs, beaten separately

2 teaspoons sugar

1 teaspoon salt

4 tablespoons butter

Preheat the oven to 350 degrees. Bring to a boil one cup of the milk, add the corn and the cornmeal, stirring constantly, and cook for five minutes. Remove from the fire and beat in the butter, sugar, and salt, and the rest of the milk. The cold milk should cool the mixture. Add the beaten egg yolks, then fold in the stiffly beaten whites. Pour the mixture into a buttered dish and bake for thirty minutes.

Stuffed Cabbage

1 medium (#2) fresh cabbage

1 cup pork sausage

1 cup chopped cabbage

1 cup breadcrumbs

1 egg

1/2 teaspoon salt

Cut the whole cabbage halfway down into eight sections from the top toward the stem. Drop it into warm water for ten minutes. Fold back the sections, leaving each one four or five leaves thick. Scoop out the center, leaving an opening sufficient to hold the stuffing.

Chop the removed cabbage. Make a force meat of the remaining ingredients and fill the cabbage. Bring the sections back over the stuffing, tie the whole cabbage in cheesecloth, drop it in boiling water, and let it cook for an hour. When the cabbage is done, lift it out and drain well. Place on a platter and sprinkle with fresh parsley and serve.

Cornmeal Lace Cakes

1/2 cup ground cornmeal
2/3 cup cold water
1/4 teaspoon salt

Mix the ingredients into a thin batter. Into a heavy skillet put two or three tablespoons of lard and let it heat to a rather hot temperature without allowing it to smoke. Pour the batter into the pan, using one tablespoon to make a cake as large as the top of a small teacup. Hold the spoon two or three inches from the pan so that the batter will spatter, making a lacy cake. Brown, turn, and brown the other side. When the cakes are light brown and crisp like a water, they are ready to serve. Each one will require about two minutes cooking time. Add more lard as needed to make the cakes spatter.

When bread or cakes burn, use a grater
to remove the burned area.

Sunday Biscuits

2 1/2 cups flour
1/3 cup butter
3/4 cup milk
1 egg
4 teaspoons baking powder
1 teaspoon salt
1 tablespoon sugar

Preheat the oven to 400 degrees. Sift the sugar, salt, and baking powder with the flour. Break the egg into a cup and beat well; then fill the cup with the milk. Mix the butter into the flour, then mix into a dough with the milk-and-egg mixture, using a spoon.

Turn onto a well-floured board and knead until smooth, using extra flour, if needed. Roll out to a one-quarter-inch thickness, cut with a tea biscuit cutter, butter on one side, turn over, and place on a baking sheet. Bake for about twelve minutes.

Baking powder was not invented until 1850.

Cheese Straws

1 stick pure butter
2 cups sharp cheese, grated
1 teaspoon baking powder
1/2 teaspoon salt
1 1/2 cup sifted flour
1/4 teaspoon cayenne

Preheat the oven to 400 degrees. Cream the butter well. Add the cheese and blend. Stir in all the dry ingredients. Roll out the mixture to a thickness of about one-half inch and cut into strips about one-half inch wide. Place the strips on a baking sheet and bake for fifteen minutes or until brown. This receipt makes about four dozen straws.

Old-Fashioned Banana Nut Bread

1/2 cup pure butter, softened
1 cup sugar
2 eggs, well beaten
2 tablespoons sour milk
1 teaspoon fresh lemon juice
1/2 teaspoon baking soda

1/4 teaspoon salt

2 cups flour

4 large bananas, very ripe, mashed

1/2 cup pecans or walnuts

1 1/2 teaspoons baking powder

Preheat the oven to 350 degrees. Cream the butter, sugar, and eggs, in a large bowl. Mix well. Add all the remaining ingredients. Grease and flour a loaf pan (nine inches by five inches). Bake for about one hour or until a broom straw inserted in the center comes out clean. Let the loaf cool for about ten minutes before removing it from the pan.

Sugar Plum Pudding

1 cup four

3/4 teaspoon cinnamon

1 1/2 teaspoons nutmeg

3/4 teaspoon soda

1/2 cup fresh butter

1/4 cup sugar

1 egg, well beaten

1/2 cup buttermilk

1/2 cup prunes, cooked and chopped

Preheat the oven to 350 degrees. Mix the flour, spices, and soda. Add the butter to the dry ingredients. Add the sugar and mix well. Add the eggs and buttermilk to the prunes; then add this mixture to the dry ingredients. Mix well. Pour into a buttered pan and bake until done.

Sugar Plum Glaze

1/2 stick pure butter

1/4 cup buttermilk

1/2 cup sugar

1/4 teaspoon pure vanilla extract

Bring the butter, buttermilk, and sugar to a full rolling boil. Remove from the heat and add the vanilla extract. Pour over the pudding.

Gold and Silver Cake

GOLD CAKE

1 cup sugar
1/2 cup fresh butter
5 egg yolks
2 cups plain flour
1/2 teaspoon soda
1 teaspoon cream of tartar
1/2 cup sweet milk
1 teaspoon pure vanilla extract

Preheat the oven to 350 degrees. Cream the sugar and butter together. Add the egg yolks and beat well. Sift all the dry ingredients together and add them to the batter, alternating them with the milk. Add the vanilla. Cook in two greased eight-inch layer tins until the layers turn loose from the edges of the pan and a broom straw inserted into the center of the layers comes out clean.

SILVER CAKE

1/2 cup butter
1 1/2 cups sugar
1 teaspoon cream of tartar
1/2 teaspoon soda
3 cups flour
1 cup sweet milk
1 teaspoon pure vanilla extract
6 egg whites

Cream the butter and sugar together. Add the dry ingredients to the creamed mixture, alternating with the milk and the vanilla. Beat the egg whites to a froth and fold them into the batter. Cook in three eight-inch cake pans, greased and lightly floured, until the layers turn loose from the edges of the pan and a broom straw inserted into the center of the layers comes out clean. The layers will be thin. Alternate one silver and gold layer until you have stacked all five layers, icing each with your favorite white icing and filling it with fresh coconut before adding the next layer.

Crystallized Roses and Mint Leaves

Delicate and perishable, the rose is one of the most ancient flowers. There are many legends about its origin. One attributes the rose to a rivalry between the sea and the earth. As Venus was born from sea foam, the shores gave birth to the rose, proving that they could create something as beautiful as Venus, the goddess of love.

When Cleopatra entertained Mark Anthony in Cilicia, she is reported to have covered the floor of the banquet hall with eighteen inches of rose petals. Nero, a man known for extremes, covered the entire surface of Lake Lucina with rose petals.

In the South during Victorian days, the "tussie-mussie" was a charming accessory of courtship. It was a bouquet of roses encased in a paper frill and pinned into a holder. A Victorian lady carried her tussie-mussie of roses from the ballroom to the altar. Afterwards, it was waxed, holder and all, and preserved under a domed glass, which was placed upon the parlor table.

2 egg whites
15 roses, barely open
30 large fresh mint leaves
2 cups granulated sugar in a bowl

Have the egg whites at room temperature and beat them until they are very foamy. Dip one rose at a time into the foam, shaking off any excess. Immediately dip the coated rose in sugar or sprinkle it with sugar. Do the mint leaves the same way.

Place the roses and mint leaves on a rack and put them in the refrigerator overnight or until they are thoroughly dry. If any of the roses and mint leaves are not covered, repeat the process, only this time use a small pastry brush and touch up the sections that are uncovered.

Sugared Pecans

1 1/2 quarts large pecans
2 1/4 cups sugar
2/3 cup water
Grated rind of 1 fresh orange

Mix the sugar and water and boil until the syrup spins a thread. Then continue cooking until the mixture reaches a soft ball stage. Remove from the heat. Add the grated orange rind and stir until it gets foamy. Stir in the shelled pecans, carefully coating each one well. Pour into a lightly greased dish and separate with the tines of a fork while the syrup is still warm. Let the pecans harden and cool.

Sweet Potato Pudding

1 cup butter
1 cup sugar
6 egg yolks
3 teaspoons pure brandy
1 teaspoon ginger
1 teaspoon allspice
1 teaspoon cinnamon
1 fresh lemon, juice and rind
2 1/2 cups sweet potatoes, cooked
6 egg whites

Preheat the oven to 350 degrees. Cream the butter and sugar together, add the egg yolks, and beat. Mix in the other ingredients, except the egg whites. Beat the whites until they are light and frothy. Fold them into the potato mixture and bake for about forty-five minutes.

Rich, Tender Hot Rolls

This receipt comes from Ashford Springs, Alabama. Around 1845 it was a fashionable watering place for the wealthy planters of Choctaw and Sumter counties. A hotel that could accommodate around two hundred guests opened in 1846. The resort was dubbed the "Saratoga of the South." One of its springs contained white sulphur, another sulphur-chalybeate, and another vichy. Today nothing remains of the resort except a marble basin at one of the springs.

1/2 cup sugar
1 teaspoon salt

3/4 cup milk

1/2 cup butter

2 packages fresh or dry yeast

1/2 cup fairly hot water

4 to 4 1/2 cups all-purpose flour

2 eggs

Combine the milk, butter, salt, and sugar in a pot and heat them until the butter dissolves. Cool to lukewarm. Dissolve the yeast in the hot water and stir. Mix approximately one-and-a-half cups of flour with the milk mixture; add the yeast and sugar. Gradually stir in the remaining flour.

Turn the dough out onto a floured board. Knead until satiny, not sticky. Cover the dough with a linen napkin and let it rise in a warm place. It should double its bulk in about one-and-a-half hours. Punch the dough down and shape it into rolls. Let the rolls rise until they are double in bulk.

Preheat the oven to 400 degrees. Bake the rolls for thirty to forty-five minutes. This receipt makes about three dozen rolls.

When the rolls are taken from the oven, they should be brushed with hot melted butter.

Fresh Peach Delight

3 cups milk

1/2 cup raw long-grain rice

1/4 teaspoon salt

3 egg yolks

1/2 teaspoon pure vanilla extract

1/2 cup granulated sugar

1/2 cup heavy cream, whipped

8 fresh peach halves

Fresh raspberries to fill peach halves

Sugar cubes

Pure lemon extract

In the top of a double-boiler, combine the milk, rice, and salt, and bring them to a boil, stirring constantly. Then over hot water cook, covered, for about forty minutes or until all the milk is absorbed by the rice.

Combine the egg yolks, vanilla, and sugar; stir this mixture into the rice mixture. Cook, stirring, for about five minutes longer. Then refrigerate the pudding until it is well chilled.

Fold in the whipped cream and spoon into individual dishes, filling each about two-thirds full. Sprinkle with nutmeg. On top of each serving, arrange a peach half, hollow side up. Spoon fresh raspberries into each peach half and place a sugar cube dipped in lemon extract over the berries. Light with a match and serve at once.

Herbed New Potatoes

1 1/2 pounds new potatoes
4 tablespoons pure butter, melted
1 tablespoon lemon juice
3 tablespoons parsley, snipped
1 tablespoon fresh chives, chopped
2 heads fresh dill, snipped
Dash salt
Dash white pepper

Scrub the potatoes with a coarse brush. Pare a strip around the center of each potato. Cook the potatoes in boiling, salted water for twenty-five minutes. Drain and return the potatoes to the pan. Combine the butter, lemon juice, and herbs. Stir this mixture into the potatoes and coat them thoroughly. This receipt makes about six servings.

Real Deep-Dish Apple Pie with Cheese Crust

This receipt is supposed to have been brought over on the *Mayflower* in 1620.

3 cups very tart apples
1 cup sugar
1/2 teaspoon nutmeg
Dribble cinnamon

1 tablespoon lemon juice

1 handful chopped citron

1/4 pound pure butter

Preheat the oven to 400 degrees. Be sure that the apples are very tart, as eating apples do not make a good pie. Peel the apples and slice them very thin. Roll out the bottom crust (receipt follows) and line an earthen dish with it. Spread one-half cup sugar evenly over the bottom of the crust. Arrange the sliced apples in the dish, piling them as high as possible.

Sprinkle the remaining one-half cup of sugar over the apples, then add the nutmeg, cinnamon, lemon juice, and citron. Cut the butter into bits over the apples and spices.

Roll out the top crust, place it over the fruit, and make a slit in the top to allow steam to escape. Wet the edges of the upper and lower crusts enough to press them together. Seal them well because the pie will be ruined if the juice escapes.

Brown quickly in the hot oven, then reduce the heat to 300 degrees and cook slowly for one hour. When the pie is baked, the apples will be translucent and tender, and the juice will be like jelly.

The success of this pie depends in large measure upon your using an earthen dish for cooking.

CHEESE CRUST

2 cups all-purpose flour

1/2 teaspoon salt

Dash cayenne pepper

1/2 cup pure lard

1/4 pound sharp cheese, grated

7 tablespoons ice water

Vegetable oil

Egg white

Sift the dry ingredients and cut in the shortening until the mixture is rather mealy. Mix cheese in lightly. Add the ice water gradually, making a stiff dough. Roll out on a floured board and place in an earthen dish. Brush the inside crust with vegetable oil very lightly and the top crust with egg white. This will make the crust crisp and beautifully brown.

There is a story about a boy and pies that has survived a long time. It was written in 1907 by Sara Cone Bryant. She tells the tale of a little boy named Epaminendas. It seemed that he could never do anything right. One day his mammy warned him, "You mind now, Epaminendas, how you step in those pies set out on the back steps to cool!" Epaminendas listened to his mammy very carefully and stepped right in the middle of each and every pie!

Coffee Caramel Candy

1 1/2 cups real cream
1 cup granulated sugar
1/2 cup brown sugar
1/2 cup light corn syrup
4 tablespoons pure butter
2 tablespoons strong freshly brewed coffee
1 teaspoon pure vanilla extract
Speck salt

Butter the sides and bottom of a large pan. In a saucepan combine the cream, sugars, corn syrup (molasses was used by earlier cooks), butter, salt, and coffee. Cook stirring constantly over a low heat until the sugar dissolves. Cook over a medium heat, stirring less frequently, until the candy reaches a firm ball stage (248 degrees with a candy thermometer). Remove from the heat and stir in the vanilla. Turn into a buttered pan. This will make a batch of around three dozen candies.

Divinity Candy Divine

2 cups pure maple syrup
1/4 teaspoon salt
1/2 cup unbroken pecans
2 egg whites

Butter the sides of a heavy saucepan and cook the syrup rapidly over a high heat to the hard ball stage (250 degrees on a candy thermometer) without stirring. Remove from the heat. At once add the salt to the egg whites and beat them to very stiff peaks. Pour the hot syrup slowly over the stiff egg whites, beating constantly, as fast as you can. Beat until the mixture forms soft peaks and begins to lose its gloss. Add the nuts and drop by teaspoons onto a buttered pan.

Watermelon Sweetmeats

Watermelon rind, peeled and cut into small pieces
2 1/2 cups sugar per pound of rind
2 lemons per five pounds of rind
Alum
Salt

Peel and remove all ripe red from the rind. Cut the rind into small squares. Soak for twelve hours in salted water, using one tablespoon of salt for each quart of water. Drain on a linen towel. Cover with fresh water and boil for about twenty minutes, adding a pinch of alum. Drain again on a linen towel. Boil the sugar with water, using one cup of sugar to each three-quarters cup of water, until a thin syrup is formed. Add the rind and sliced lemon and let the mixture cook until the rind is tender and translucent. Pour into sterilized jars and seal.

Indian Peach Pickle

There is a small peach grown in Alabama that is red on the outside and yellow on the inside. It makes a beautiful pickle and seldom do you find it missing from a Sunday dinner table in the South.

7 pounds peaches, peeled
Cloves
3 1/2 pounds brown sugar
3 cups vinegar
1 teaspoon salt
2 tablespoons allspice

2 tablespoons cloves
2 thick sticks cinnamon

Peel the peaches. Stick two whole cloves in each peach. Combine the sugar, vinegar, salt, and spices in a large kettle. Bring the mixture to a boil. Put in about ten or twelve peaches at a time and cook slowly until they are tender enough to be pierced with a broom straw. Remove the cooked peaches and cook the syrup over moderate heat for about fifteen minutes until it is thick. Pack the peaches in sterilized jars and pour syrup over them.

Glossary of Herbs, Spices, and Flavorings Used in *Sook's Cookbook*

Fresh herbs are particularly aromatic just after they have been watered and the sun is shining on their foliage. What makes the plant release its pungent fragrance through the air and onto the fingers is a mist of almost invisible drops of oil on every leaf.

Sook had her own herb garden, and cooking in the Fault house was done, whenever possible, with her fresh herbs. She loved the stories and legends about the herbs, spices, and flavorings she grew and used, and I have collected a few of them here, along with some practical information about these important additions to many recipes.

Basil: This small bushy plant has leaves of golden green, with a hint of chartreuse. At times the foliage glistens with deeply scented drops of oil. The smell has hints of cloves, licorice, and tree-ripened oranges.

In the olden days it was believed that basil could make a person have a merry heart. Women in labor sometimes held a sprig of basil in their hands, along with the feather of a swallow, to ensure that their babies would be born without pain.

Basil is a sacred herb in India, where it is believed that a leaf placed on the breast of a Hindu at death will be his special key to heaven.

Some old-time mammies in the South still believe that a basil plant will keep flies out of a room.

Cardamon: This spice is very old and aromatic. Records show that it was grown in the garden of the king of Babylon in 721 B.C. It is a member of the ginger family and is native to India and Ceylon. It grows and flourishes in warm rain forests.

The cardamon plant begins to bear fruit in its fourth year and will continue to do so for many years. The fruits or capsules are harvested while they are still green and only about three-quarters ripe.

Each cardamom capsule contains about twenty dark-brown aromatic seeds. The outer capsule cover has no flavor and will range in color from green to white, depending on the variety. The drying method often determines the final color. "Greens" are dried artificially in kilns or rooms with forced hot air and, therefore, retain some of their natural color. Lighter-colored capsules have usually been dried in the sun. Sometimes cardamom is treated with sulphur to bleach it a pure white.

Malabar cardamom is considered the best for cooking.

Chives: Chives flourish wild in Greece, England, and Italy, as well as in many other places. Chives were used at least two thousand years ago as a remedy for bleeding. Like onions, they are rich in sulphur, and sometimes chives are referred to as the little brother of the onion.

An extra bonus to the delightful flavor of the plant and its fresh appearance are its lavender pompom flowers that appear each spring.

It is said that the early Dutch settlers in this country planted chives in their pastures so that their cows would give chive-flavored milk.

Coriander: The Chinese consider coriander their own precious green seasoning and refer to it as Chinese parsley. You must be chary of fresh coriander, as the feathery green tips must be used sparingly. Always use this spice with caution. The seeds lose their unpleasant odor when they are dried and have a mild, pleasant orange flavor. It is not wise to grow coriander indoors because of its unpleasant smell.

Dill: This plant is native to the shores of the Mediterranean and to southern Russia. Its name comes from an ancient Norse word, *dilla,* meaning "to lull," and a decoction made from dill was sometimes fed to babies to lull them to sleep. Our early American ancestors referred to dill as "meeting seeds" and nibbled on them during church in order to catch a catnap during long, boring sermons.

In the olden days, brides used to put a sprig of dill in their shoes with a dash of salt, and they would wear a spray of the herb as well, both for good luck.

Garlic: No real cook in the Deep South can do without garlic. Garlic and onions are among the oldest known cultivated plants. Garlic was part of the daily ration given to the slaves who worked on the great pyramid of Cheops in Egypt.

It is hard to believe that garlic is a member of the lily family. The lilies, hyacinths, tulips, and other fragrant members of this family must want to deny the relationship to smelly garlic, by far the raunchiest, boldest, least fragrant lily of them all. But due to the plant's boldness, the world has been unable to ignore garlic, which is now adored all over the globe.

Ginger: The ancient Chinese and Hindus grew ginger for use as both a spice and a medicine. Marco Polo claimed to have discovered it in China, but authorities say that the builders of the Egyptian pyramids ate sweet unleavened ginger cakes before Marco Polo's journey. A Greek baker in Rhodes in 240 B.C. is credited with making the world's first gingerbread.

Mace: Mace is unique in that it grows on the same plant as another spice, nutmeg. They are the only two distinct varieties of spice growing in that way. Male and female trees grow separately, but only the fertilized female trees bear fruit. When the fruit on the tree ripens, it splits in half. Inside can be found a wrinkled brown nut covered by a scarlet net-like membrane, called the aril. This aril is mace, while the kernel found inside the brown shell is nutmeg.

Marjoram: Marjoram grows wild on the hillsides of Asia and along the borders of the Mediterranean. The leaves are gray-green, oval in shape, and velvety.

According to an old legend, this plant was raised by the goddess Venus on the shores of one of the Greek islands. When Venus first planted marjoram, it had no scent, but from the constant magic touch of the goddess, it soon caught its fragrance.

Mint: Legend says that Pluto, lord of the underworld, loved a beautiful nymph named Minthe. Proserpine, his jealous wife, changed Minthe into the herb now known as mint. Because of its bracing and clean aroma, mint came to be used to perfume bath water and as a strewing herb.

Some of the common mints used in our country today are: apple mint, white mint, lemon mint, pineapple mint, pennyroyal, Corsican mint, curly mint, watermint, and bergamot.

Unquenchable in their enthusiasm for growing, mints are flamboyant and fascinating. When you find them they flourish in great sweeps, the roots woven together as thick as mats.

The Pilgrim fathers packed mint with their chickens, breadfruits, and other treasures they brought with them when they sailed for America. The varieties of this plant are legion, and its uses are practically uncountable.

Breathing the essence of mint clears the head and quickens and arouses the sense.

Nutmeg: See the entry on mace (above) for additional information about nutmeg's unusual growth circumstances.

Once nutmeg has been grated, it loses its strength and pungency very quickly.

In olden days gentlemen often carried their personal nutmeg graters with them when they dined out or traveled.

Olives: Every Bible reader knows that this oleaginous fruit of the Orient has been a friend to mankind since Noah's time, when the celebrated dove, olive branch in its bill, announced the end of the flood.

The fruit of the olive tree grows in clusters, the maturing berries changing first from green to yellow, then to red, and finally ripening to a hue of deep purple or black. The taste does not sweeten as the color changes. Even the ripe berries are bitter to the tongue. The bitterness can be removed by soaking the olives in water.

Oregano: Oregano and marjoram are often confused with each other. Botanists claim that oregano is just a strain of wild marjoram, but to most cooks they remain two separate herbs.

Oregano has fairly large leaves and bears tiny pink or purple flowers. Its pungency will vary, depending on the variety and where it is grown. Oregano from Mexico is different than European oregano. In the United States, we usually use the European variety.

There is a legend regarding oregano. A servant to Cinyrasm, king of Cyprus, dropped and spilled a large vessel of perfume. Afraid of being punished, the servant fainted and was metamorphosized into oregano.

The spice was not used to a great extent in this country until around 1940. Soldiers returning from the war created a demand for oregano because they wanted to recreate the wonderful meals they remembered from Europe.

An old name for oregano was "joy of the mountain."

Parsley: There are many old tales about parsley. One blames the plant's slow germination on the fact that it has to go to the devil and come back again nine times before it sprouts. Another tale says that a pregnant woman's planting the herb will speed up the germination process.

Pepper: Long considered the world's most important spice, pepper is the small, round berry of a woody vine native to the Malabar coast of India. Spice merchants during the Middle Ages were called *poiviers* in French, pepperers in English, and *pieffersacke* in German.

Both black and white pepper come from the same berry. The difference comes form when they berry is picked and how it is treated. Black pepper is picked when the berries are still green, before they ripen. They are piled up and allowed to sit and ferment for a few days before they are dried. The peppercorns will shrivel up and turn black or brown-black in color.

White pepper is picked once the berries have ripened, when they are green-yellow in color and just before they turn red. These berries are soaked in water for about eight or nine days, then the soft outer pericarp (hull) is removed. When dried, these berries turn white.

Subtle differences between black and white pepper exist. Black peppercorns have a more robust aroma while white pepper has a stronger flavor. Some cooks find that three parts black peppercorns to two parts white peppercorns to one part allspice berries produces a mixture with an excellent flavor and aroma.

Rosemary: This plant is tall and shiny and bears blossoms of the palest blue. It is said that rosemary blossoms get their heavenly blue because Mary hung her blue coat on a rosemary bush when the Holy Family stopped to rest during their flight to Egypt. Rosemary is sacred to remembrance and friendship, and legend says that it will not thrive in the garden of one who is not just and righteous. If your rosemary does not flourish, take a good look at yourself.

Sassafras: In the Deep South we are blessed with plenty of sassafras. Filé (pronounced fee-*lay*) is the finely ground leaves of sassafras. These leaves should be gathered during the month of August, during the full moon. They should be broken from the branches of the tree and hung to dry in a shaded, ventilated place for about two weeks. The sun should shine on the leaves for at least an hour or two before they are ground. Store the filé in amber jars, tightly sealed, in a cool place.

Summer Savory: A native of the Mediterranean region, summer savory, according to the ancients, was a favorite of the wanton satyrs and woodland deities, who wore wreaths of the plant as crowns. During the summer, tiny pale lavender and pink flowers appear like raindrops all through the foliage. This herb adds a wonderful flavor to fresh beans.

Old-timers believe that savory heated with oil of roses and dripped into the ears would cure deafness.

Index